Raise the Bar

Zero to 1 Billion: Combining Lean and Digital for People-Centric, Sustainable Growth

Michael Ballé, Nicolas Chartier,
Guillaume Paoli, Régis Medina

Foreword by Daniel Jones

 **KEENLY**PRESS

Copyright © 2022 by
Michael Ballé, Nicolas Chartier,
Guillaume Paoli, Régis Medina

Cover and book design by Charlotte Bayart
and book layout by Mélanie Luciani

Printed in the United States of America

First Printing: June 2022

ISBN: 978-2-9583570-0-9

CONTENTS

CHAPTER 12:
RAISE THE BAR _____ 321

CHAPTER 13:
PERFORMANCE IS PERSONAL _____ 335

CHAPTER 14:
SHARE INNOVATION _____ 361

CHAPTER 15:
WHAT WE KNOW NOW _____ 381

CONCLUSION _____399

FOREWORD

aise the bar! This remarkable book relates how a digital start-up sustained its momentum through the critical scale-up phase: Drawing inspiration from the lean strategy that powered Toyota to becoming the largest car company in the world. Describing the journey from the perspective of the founder determined to succeed and his sensei, or teacher, who kept on asking searching questions. Sharing how their thinking changed as they found and faced up to problem after problem encountered by employees. And how they created a culture of engagement and problem-solving. It is a microcosm of any business facing challenging times.

Although growing profits are a signal of success, this story is important for three reasons. First, it was not based on telling employees what to do, but on encouraging them to discover what problems need to be addressed and giving them the methodology and support to do so themselves. This people-centric approach builds capabilities through "learning by problem-solving." In the scramble for talent, retaining these capabilities will be critical to continuing to grow and prosper.

Second, this story shows that the ultimate success of new ideas depends on rapid and sustained problem-solving through successive product generations. Rapid scaling up that is built on customer and employee experience and explores all the technical possibilities is key. In the end, this will distinguish the winners from the losers.

Third, this story also shows how problem-solving capabilities and rapid scale-up are just what are needed to respond to the climate crisis and to recycling in the circular economy – particularly in discovering and experimenting with different ways of tackling new problems no one yet knows how to solve. Framing these problems as gaps to be closed prioritizes actions. This gives leaders the confidence to put this at the heart of their strategy, rather than dragging their feet to protect existing assets.

Raise the Bar is a truly unique book from which every executive can draw valuable lessons for their own journey. It will change the way you think about business strategy.

DANIEL JONES,
ROSS-ON-WYE

ACKNOWLEDGMENTS

Warm thanks to Cyril Gras for his effective project management (as well as being a key protagonist of the story), George Taninecz for his production skill, Mélanie Luciani for her stylish layout, Charlotte Bayart for her elegant cover design, and Brian Frastaci for his careful copyediting.

This story is really the story of all the great people that have made Aramis Group a success, and we want to express our deepest gratitude for their commitment and contributions over the years. A heartfelt thank-you in particular to Romain Boscher, Wim Bruggeman, Ivo Willems, Steve Butterley, Philip Wilkinson, Pablo Fernández, Carlos Rivera, and José-Carlos del Valle and their teams. We know gembas are sometimes challenging times, and we are thrilled to learn together!

A big thank-you to the teams who helped us start this learning journey in France: Anne-Claire Baschet, Fabrice Farcot, Guillaume Limare, Brigitte Schifano, Alejandro Garcia-Mella, Rémi Pigeol, Jean-Michel Berthelier, Thomas Koell, Zakaria Bouzekri, Frédérik

Le Gac, Juliette Dumas, Khadija Boussairi, Clémence Roynette, and Antoine Vicquery.

We would also like to give deep thanks to our mentors in this journey: Freddy Ballé, Jacques Chaize, Orry Fiume, Daniel Jones, Marc Onetto, Marcus Chao, Joe Lee and Isao Yoshino, our lean sensei. Lean is a collective endeavor, and we are grateful for all the fruitful exchanges we've had with other lean CEOs and lean coaches in our study trips in Japan: Arnaud Barde, Siham Bentalab, Fabrice Bernhard, Jean-Claude Bihr, Jean-Baptiste Bouthillon, Catherine Chabiron, Benoit Charles-Lavauzelle, Steve Anavi, Cyril Dané, Frédéric Fiancette, Philippe Grosse, Nicolas Guillemet, Sandrine Olivencia, Daryl Powell, Eiving Reke, Christophe Riboulet, Christophe Richard, Cécile Roche, Anne-Lise Seltzer, and our tour organizer Mami Takeda.

For their support as special advisors, we warmly thank Pierre Guénant, Alix de Poix, Nick Carbonari, and Eric Grabli. They have followed the journey from almost the beginning and know how steep the learning curve has been!

To Stellantis, for their trust as our main shareholder for the last six years, Carlos Tavares, Philippe de Rovira, Marc Lechantre, Lucie Vigier, Philip Robson, and Jean-Baptiste de Chatillon.

Most of all, we would like to thank our families for their staunch support in the ups and downs of both writing a book and growing a business: Florence, Roman and Alexandre, Mathilde, Adèle, Louise and Malo, Charlotte, Victoire, Côme and Apolline, Séverine, Chloé, and Romeo and Tom.

We also would like to thank the 500,000 customers in all of Europe that have trusted us to purchase or sell their cars, with special thanks to our very first customer back in 2001, Mrs. Paunet!

AUTHORS

Michael Ballé, PhD, is a business writer, executive coach, and organizational researcher. He has studied lean transformations for the past 30 years and helped CEOs to grow their own lean cultures. He is the coauthor of the bestselling Gold Mine trilogy (*The Gold Mine*,[1] *The Lean Manager*,[2] and *Lead with Respect*[3]), *The Lean Strategy*,[4] *The Lean Sensei*,[5] *Lead with Lean*,[6] and other titles. His work has been translated into 10 languages and has received four Shingo Research and Publication awards. He is the cofounder of Institut Lean France and Business Dynamics collection director at L'Harmattan.

Nicolas Chartier is cofounder of Aramis Group, formed in 2001; coauthor of *The Lean Sensei*;[5] and a graduate of the Kedge Business School of Bordeaux.

[1] F. Ballé & M. Ballé (2005). *The Gold Mine*, Lean Enterprise Institute, Brookline, MA.

[2] F. Ballé & M. Ballé (2009). *The Lean Manager*, Lean Enterprise Institute, Cambridge, MA.

[3] F. Ballé & M. Ballé (2014). *Lead with Respect*, Lean Enterprise Institute, Cambridge, MA.

[4] M. Ballé, J. Chaize, O. Fiume, & D. Jones (2017). *The Lean Strategy*, McGraw Hill, New York.

[5] M. Ballé, P. Bierma, N. Chartier, P. Coignet, D. Powell, S. Olivencia, & E. Reke (2020). *The Lean Sensei*, Lean Enterprise Institute, Boston.

[6] M. Ballé (2016). *Lead with Lean*.

He began his career at Vinexpo, a company that organizes events for international operators in the wines and spirits sectors, as manager of the Hong Kong office. In 1999, he held the position of export zone manager of Africa and the Middle East at the Baron Philippe de Rothschild company, which operates in the wine market. From 2000 to 2001, he served as chief executive officer of SEBO.

Guillaume Paoli, cofounder of Aramis Group, holds a degree in marketing from the ESSEC Business School in Paris. From 1997 to 1999, he worked as European new brands project head and brand manager with Unilever, a global leader in the consumer products market. He then served as marketing director for SEBO from 2000 to 2001. Since 2018, he has been a member of the board of directors of Brigad, an innovative start-up that connects workers and companies, allowing them to instantaneously find the best profiles for periodic tasks. He also has been a member since 2014 of the strategy committee of RAISE France, a venture capital company and endowment fund that aims to promote the impact economy and philanthropic finance.

Régis Medina was one of the early pioneers of agile methodologies in the late 1990s. In 2009, he embarked on a journey to explore the practices of Toyota, eventually making several trips to Japan. At the same time, he works with more than 100 teams to adapt this model to modern tech companies. Regis now works with prominent entrepreneurs of the French tech community to build fast-growing, highly adaptative scale-ups.

INTRODUCTION

I n June 2021, we introduced our company at the Euronext stock exchange in one of its largest initial public offerings. Twenty years ago, we'd started what has become Aramis Group with a phone and a laptop in Nicolas' studio, 10 days after 9/11 and a few months after the internet bubble had burst. We were passionate about cars, and our plan was to use the possibilities of the budding web (this was before Amazon had branched out of books) to turn how people bought cars on its head. At that time, car sales were organized purely for the manufacturer's convenience, and we thought we could do better than that by focusing on customer needs and taking away the (many) pain points in the buying process.

On the way, we came across what would turn out to be one of the greatest challenges of our times: developing a circular economy to reduce the pressure on the planet. As we followed our customers' wishes, we learned that they increasingly looked for sharing, leasing, and, strikingly, purchasing refurbished secondhand cars. In order to control quality and the value creation chain, we set up our first reconditioning plant in France and are now in the process of expanding these activities across Europe. As we grew up as a business, what started as a purely pragmatic response to people's wishes has become a firm commitment to contributing to a different form of automotive market and consumption.

Success colors every winning journey with rose-tinted glasses, but, as we all know, the real path is strewn with surprising challenges through which we must see our way, finding the right responses in order to progress and prevail. The story we want to tell is how we knew scaling up the company would bring serious challenges, on the customer satisfaction front as well as on our operational capacities (both are intimately linked), and how we struggled through trial and error to figure out how to respond. We knew it was coming, we knew what we wanted the company to be like, but we didn't know how to reach our destination.

"Learn or die" was our mantra when we started the company in 2001, and, like most successful start-ups, we had a slow start and then fast growth. In 2007, we had some buzz as the next "gazelle," to take David Birch's term, because of our hypergrowth. But then, after a decade of working like crazy just to keep up with demand, growth started to slow – something we had expected and feared. We refinanced and spent all we could on marketing to restart the growth engine. At this stage, to the business world, we were a solid success story. Internally, we knew we were in trouble. Our marketing costs and overheads were increasing faster than our turnover. We had trouble keeping up with customers and were disappointing too many people. Most of our energy went into constant firefighting due to endless internal issues, and this started to take its toll – we were losing good people. The most frustrating part about this is that we realized what was happening – we talked about it endlessly – but couldn't seem to find a smart way to sidestep the issue.

Our start-up strategy has been to use digital techniques to eliminate customer pain points – and then to industrialize the reconditioning process to control quality and deliver to the growing demand for good-as-new, secondhand cars. Some of these pain points we could get rid of completely, such as the stress of negotiating with a car salesman by offering a low, nonnegotiable price on our website. Some we tried hard to mitigate, such as helping customers choose a car across brands in our virtual, multibrand showroom rather than have to physically visit dealership after dealership to compare models in the same range. We found the lean promise of "total elimination of waste" intuitive and promising, as it sounded close enough to our idea of "pain points" – widening the pain points concept from customers to employees and suppliers.

Looking for answers, in 2012 we started a lean experiment with a single consultant. It was interesting but inconclusive. We then pursued more changes with specialized lean consultants and achieved visible results, but they wouldn't hold.

Still, we invested in our own lean program with a lean office and projects to eliminate waste from our processes. Some of these projects were very successful, demonstrating significant results; but the performance improvements were hard to maintain, our already over-burdened people complained of the increase in workload from yet more projects, and by 2016 the overall situation wasn't getting any better. We saw the potential – highlighted by the projects' successes – but also saw how the organization's weight would revert any initiative to the mean very quickly. Interestingly, we were the only ones to think there *really* was a problem – from a purely financial point of view, the company was doing well. We had a decent (not great) EBITDA and had just refinanced very successfully. And that's just the point – we were worried sick about the nonfinancial aspects of the business, those that don't appear in the rear-view mirror of managing by the numbers. We struggled to deliver to customers as we would have liked, the website glitched, our internal systems bugged, employees were stressed. We looked ahead, down the road, and did not like what we saw.

We'd learned from experience that market conditions impacted our profitability almost instantly (we buy and sell cars, so our spot margin mainly depends on whether people are buying cars or not and whether the market is flooded with overproduction or not), but internal decisions and policy changes take one to two years to appear in the financials. We were scratching our heads to find ways to do things differently. We were trying to implement lean logistics in our supply chain, without much success. Running the business was becoming frustrating, as many attempts to fix our problems seemed to run into the ground.

At that point, we finally followed the first piece of advice of all the lean books we had read: find a sensei you can work with. "Sensei" is a lean term for expert/

veteran/coach – it doesn't really translate, as it is neither a consultant nor a coach nor a trainer, but more like a martial arts master, someone who can help you practice lean rather than implement lean. When we finally found one and he agreed to meet us, we presented our lean program. With 25 years' experience with lean, could he help us get it right? "You can't get it right," he said. "No one can."

We didn't understand. "It's not the program – it's you," he continued. "Your misunderstandings about what lean is. Lean is not a program to improve one process after the other. It's a growth strategy to satisfy customers by developing people who deliver more value: more quality, less costs." This wasn't quite what we expected, but it did seem to fit our problem. When we insisted that this was the lean we were keen to learn, he asked: "First, are you in this to win? Or just to stay in the game?"

We were in this to win, we assured him. We really sought to change how people buy cars by facilitating their purchases; and we sought to grow the business sustainably and profitably. "And what about your people?" he asked. The aim of lean, he shared with us, is to align:

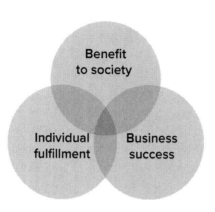

That gave us pause. From day one, we wanted to build a different sort of company, one where people could both realize their ambitions and grow the business, and we'd invested a lot of time and effort in HR programs to do so. But as with our lean initiatives, we had to admit that in the end we were growing into a normal company, where people became "human resources" and without any specific plan to link their success to our success.

"Second," the sensei continued, "are you ready to learn, or are you looking for alibi projects in order to maintain the organization's status quo?" We affirmed that we were ready to change anything we need to – we'd done that soon enough in the past. "Good," he said. "But are you ready to change your own way of thinking?"

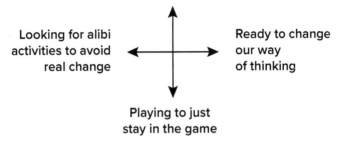

Playing to win
Finding a path to success

Looking for alibi
activities to avoid
real change

Ready to change
our way
of thinking

Playing to just
stay in the game

This conversation was definitely not going the way we'd thought it would – but we were intrigued. What kind of change? Traditional business, he explained, assumes that the only purpose of an enterprise is to make money. This requires motivating people and marketing to customers.

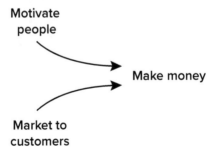

Motivate people

Make money

Market to customers

Lean, he argued, means thinking upside down: you start with an obsession with growing your customer base, so you engage all people in improving quality and reducing costs, and you make money from eliminating waste:

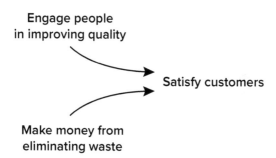

We easily saw the sense of that and said that we agreed. "But what does this concretely involve?" we asked.

"I don't know," he answered. "But I know where to look. And it starts by investigating customer complaints at the workplace. Where do you want to start?"

With hindsight, this first lesson in lean turned out to be one of the deepest – and one we need to revisit daily. Lean techniques are a *starting point*, not an end point. We don't know what the answer will be.

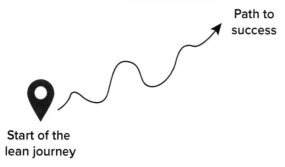

As we were to discover time and time again in concrete situations, we all have an opinion about what the answer *should be*, but the simple truth is that *we don't know* – and we need to find out. We could commit to explore rather than simply pledge to "fix" everything that was not working. Contrary to what we'd assumed with our previous lean attempts, lean practices don't have efficiency built in: they reveal problems so that people can come together, explore more deeply, and learn to discover new *knowledge points* in order to eventually change the process so the problem does not come up anymore.

At the time, we had no idea of what we were getting into. We couldn't see how committing to regular visits of our operations' workplace, the "gemba" in lean terms (meaning the real place where real work is done by real people), would solve in any way our scale-up problems. But we felt we had tried about everything else, so we were ready to attempt a leap of faith. Having disrupted the cozy business of car dealerships with our internet offer, we knew that the solutions to problems cannot be found in the thinking that created the problem in the first place. The sensei argued – and we agreed – that piling on processes to control processes would burden the business with additional costs and demand additional attention from people, further muddying priorities. We were ready to start learning again – what, we didn't know, but we were curious to *find out.*

CHAPTER 1:
DIGITAL MAGIC

igital is a kind of magic. The smartphone in your hand is like a magic wand. At a touch, you can summon a car, make an object appear at your doorstep, find out rare information, or share your thoughts. We were lucky. In the early 2000s, we saw the potential of that magic and applied it to car purchasing. Imagine if you could make one of the largest purchases in your life at the touch of a thumb. Scroll the website, find the car you want, buy it, get it delivered to your doorstep. Today, we're not there yet, as many of the steps are still too complicated to achieve in one click, but we've got the essential bricks in place, down to one of our latest innovations: home delivery.

But as we discovered the hard way, the magic of digital is the magic of the *Wizard of Oz:* there is machinery behind the curtain. To be delivered at your doorstep, the car needs to be acquired, transported, inspected, refurbished if it's a preowned car, and delivered. Then the paperwork needs to be done. Also, the digital systems themselves need to be programed, maintained, evolved. All of this is more engineering than wizardry. As we found out, it's easy to do badly, and very hard to do well. It's easy to do wastefully by throwing capital and resources at the problem, and hard to do sustainably by growing revenue faster than expenses.

Start-ups are all the rage. They're fun, they're sexy, they're exciting. And nine out of 10 start-ups will fail.[7] This point is so self-evident that Silicon Valley has turned it into its own mantra: fail fast. We were aware of the high failure rates of start-ups in growing the business and were careful to stay close to our market, to surround ourselves with leaders in the field, and to listen carefully to their (not always pleasant) advice. Indeed, we were grateful for their insights into the automotive market. We've always managed the business with a cash-first perspective – we started with 20,000 euros each, and we raised funds eight years after inception. We adopted the lean start-up methodology to build, measure, and learn on features and pivot early rather than late. All in all, we felt that we'd sufficiently nav-

[7] E. Griffith (September 25, 2014). "Why startups fail, according to their founders," *Fortune.* https://fortune.com/2014/09/25/why-startups-fail-according-to-their-founders/

igated the dangerous waters of growing the business from a "just us" start-up to a "real" business with sales points, customers, employees, and so on. Our current issues had to do with scale more than growth.

Size matters, and, ironically, success in growing to a certain size is the very cause of failure. In a nutshell, we grew because we learned, and we learned as we grew. Learn or die – this is the imperative we had given ourselves, and, indeed, we were surrounded with interesting ideas, from agile to lean start-up, to help us with that. In start-up mode, we just tried things until they worked. When we encountered an obstacle, we chipped at it by looking for any way in until an opening appeared and we could crack it, as most entrepreneurs do. In the process, we learned from our mistakes, and most of our standards were elaborated from these mistakes. Also, we learned to use all resources at hand not to solve a problem, but to find a way in. But we didn't know how to scale learning. When the company got bigger, we failed repeatedly at teaching these two basics to our staff, mostly because of our own command-and-control approach to management.

We didn't understand at first that giving a method to apply to someone didn't teach them the history of mistakes that had forged the method in the first place: more often than not, they didn't understand why the method was necessary and what it did. Most people join a company to do a specific job in a specific way, and we grew very frustrated when people did not behave as entrepreneurs would, shaking the tree and bending rules until problems got solved. With hindsight, we now can see we had people in a catch-22: apply standards, unless you have a problem, then think outside the box until you find a way around it. As a result, as the company grew, we became increasingly isolated from specific issues – customers, code, bugs. We were encouraged by mainstream thinking around us to take a step back, see the big picture, and delegate. On the flip side, we saw that people in the company did not learn as fast as the early days, nor were they likely to. They were there to do the job as it was given to them.

Our answer to the challenge of scale was *features*. Features would allow us to differentiate from traditional retailing as well as convince investors we were developing a structural competitive advantage on our market. First, customer features: to convince more customers to adopt our service, we developed new features that were supposed to help with customer acquisition. Second, internally: to support our staff, we built new features in our internal systems to help them deal with a larger range of work situations. This thinking was largely validated by the current myth that all that matters is growth, and as long as you can find funding, just keep going with customer acquisition and the rest will take care of itself. The trouble is that doing things badly means doing more things badly until customer service suffers, and customers abandon the brand for more reliable alternatives – in our case, either traditional dealerships or new entrants. On the other hand, doing things well at every step results in customer satisfaction as well as sustainable profitability. What we couldn't see clearly at the time was that our solution – adding new features – was also the cause of the resistance we felt from the business and the reason we couldn't get things to work the way we'd like.

After 10 years of breakneck growth and just adding systems and capacity to catch up to customers' growing demand for choosing cars on our website, as early as 2010 we felt that we were struggling with new car sales and that quality of service was deteriorating.

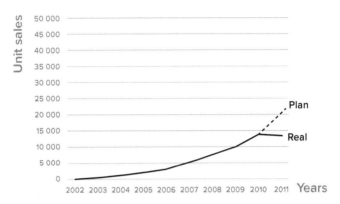

Unit sales from 2002 to 2011

We were also experiencing difficulties with the paperwork due in part to changes in the government's administrative process, and as our growth slowed, we knew we had to rethink and do something different – but what? Learning is hard enough when the solution is known and you have to master it. But we had to learn how to learn: to discover *what* needed to be learned first.

We *knew* businesses lose their customer focus as they scale – which is why we wanted to keep delivering great new features to our customers, to keep responding to their needs. We also knew companies lose their people touch as they grow, building a bureaucracy to support increasingly complex processes – which is why we wanted to offer new systems to our people so that they could retain their autonomy in doing their jobs. This is what we'd done as a start-up. We were lucky to early on recognize the immense potential of digital applied to a huge market such as automotive retail. As we looked at the car sales business, with its traditional brand dealerships and car salesmen, we had recognized four large digital opportunities: *simplify, connect, automate,* and *predict.* These helped us to steadily grow the business, but could they scale it up?

SIMPLIFY

We started the business on a simple idea: buying a car should be a delightful experience. After all, how often does anyone get the opportunity to spend so much on themselves? But from what we saw and what people told us, it was quite the opposite. Buying a car was often something of a traumatic experience. First, you had to deal with a car dealer – and fear being cheated (everyone likes to buy, no one likes to be sold to) – and second, you had to choose the right car, which was a pain because every brand throws advertisement over advertisement your way and it's very hard to know what is what. And then you had to deal with the cumbersome and annoying paperwork involved with actually owning a car.

Our first step was to remove the price negotiation from the equation. We proposed a low fixed price for the car, the same whether you purchased from our website, by phone, or at a brick-and-mortar sales point. Doing so massively simplified the purchasing process for buyers, eliminating the pain of having to negotiate with a professional who does this all day long and whose livelihood depends on how much money he squeezes out of you. Fixed prices also allowed us to undercut the competition by offering lower prices and greater sales productivity. Typically, where a retail salesperson would on average sell 10 cars a month, our sales staff would sell closer to 25. This feature was immediately successful and brought many customers right from the start.

Second, not being tied to one specific brand nor having to display the cars in a showroom, we could simplify the exploration phase of the purchasing process by showing all the brands on one site and making it easier for the prospective buyer to find something closer to their unique needs. We removed the hassle of having to visit showrooms brand by brand and listen to the salesman's spiel about what car he needed to move that month.

Third, we did our best to complete all the paperwork for our customers – not always easy due to regulatory barriers – by taking advantage of doing it a lot and often and digitizing some of the key steps.

We looked at the exploration, selection, negotiation, and purchase process; focused on the main pain point at each step of the process; and created a digital solution that would make the pain go away. In the early days, when Amazon was still just a bookseller and not yet the everything store, we didn't know whether people would go to the internet for such a major investment – but they did, at least for researching a car. And this is where we stepped in, online, and explained to the customer the multiple benefits of buying the "new way" from us. Just as with Amazon as they expanded out of books, we realized that trust was the essence of the business. We needed to be absolutely reliable to avoid replacing the distrust of the salesman on price with the distrust of a digital service on delivery.

CONNECT

We could connect anyone with any car. The second large opportunity we saw with digital was that we were no longer tied to having to sell the cars on hand in one showroom. Any customer could connect with any car they wanted wherever that car was physically at the time, and it would be our job to get them together. We developed a quick-and-dirty enterprise resource planning (ERP) system that enabled us to create logistical paths to move cars from their source to customers. We opened the first pick-up agency in 2003 and then gradually expanded our network to cover most of the territory.

After 10 years of selling new cars, we also connected buyer to seller and offered refurbished cars to our customers. We had planned to do so from the start, but the logistics of the car market made it technically difficult to start from scratch. As we built the capability to buy and deliver, we moved on to preowned cars, again adding a critical customer feature. In purchasing a car, we figured that the three major pain points were scrolling through thousands of online ads, meeting with the seller, and then making a decision about the reliability of the car. By adding a refurbishment node to our network, we used digital connectivity to expand quickly in the used-car market. In this, we added to the connectivity of internet ads, the actual purchasing of the car, and delivery to a sales point.

AUTOMATE

A third key dimension to digital are the many opportunities to automate repetitive processes. There are several basic activities that humans find both dull and hard. In our business, for instance, people contact us by phone or through the website and are then called back. Keeping track of whom to call and when is mind-boggling, and something an algorithm does easily and painlessly. We built a bespoke customer relationship management (CRM) system that automatically steered sales opportunities to our associates, who would then contact the customer to follow up. This ensured that customers were called back and not forgotten in the pipeline; and it simplified the work of our staff, who could now follow the orders presented by the system and respond without worrying about scheduling their calls themselves.

We also could automate offers – as we drew from a much wider lineup than did our one-brand competitors, we learned to automate what cars were on display on the site, keep up good deals and promotions, and search for similar models. This kind of work is simply too arduous or cumbersome for a human salesperson to do well, and software is the right tool to do these jobs smoothly and efficiently.

As we grew the business from a digital base, we saw many opportunities for automation that established companies find hard to pursue because they are simply not set up that way. Now that the company has grown, we understand why, as our own legacy systems make automation increasingly hard to pursue further, while opportunities still abound. For instance, we built the systems piecemeal, which unwittingly created a lot of dumb work transferring information from one system to another. We're currently focused on automating these computer-to-computer connections to take away all such cumbersome, wasteful work from the process.

PREDICT

Last, but not least, our entire business model was premised on the idea that if we dealt with more volume and variety, we should be able to better predict the market price of a car and, therefore, offer competitive prices to customers while turning a margin. We knew from the start that to convince customers to switch from purchasing cars the traditional way (from a dealer at a dealership), we needed to offer more than removing pain points: price leadership would make the difference.

Because cars are expensive items, costly to move around and to store, and transacted in very competitive markets, margins are typically thin. Better prediction of the delivery process was the key to convincing customers of:

- Competitive prices
- Interesting lineup (avoiding presenting lemons)
- Actual availability and precise delivery date

In a physical shop, when you see something in the front window you like, you go in and queue to get served. The sales assistant looks for the item you want in your size or to your specification, he or she shows it to you, and you walk away with your purchase. Queuing happens *before* you reach the counter, after which the experience is typically continuously and hopefully seamless (not that stores don't mess that up as well). In a digital store, you browse and purchase, and all the waiting happens after the purchase as the digital store brings the item to your door and responds to your complaints if it was not what you expected. Amazon understood early on that winning on the digital field meant, beyond price leadership, developing the fastest logistics imaginable and flexible customer service to make it easy for people to change their minds after the purchase. Similarly, our customers could change their minds without charge up to a fortnight after purchase or 1,000 kilometers driven (we have now increased it up to 30 days). Better predictability of the entire process is a key part of succeeding at delivering on the digital promise.

Simplify, connect, automate, and *predict* worked for us spectacularly in the early days, and our ability to find funding and to purchase systems sustained a steady growth, although it was always a mad scramble to deliver and keep customers happy. The people who joined the company were looking for adventure and doing things differently, and it was hectic, messy, and fun. Our hunch had paid off. But would it continue to do so as we grew and every process became more complex and involved?

CHAPTER 2:
MORE THAN MORE NEW FEATURES

A
s processes became more established, we found to our dismay that we did not know how to increase customer satisfaction through better performance. We found ourselves trapped in higher volumes and more dissatisfied customers, which we covered up with more advertising (we were growing fast, so the number of people who had purchased through us was growing in absolutes, which we communicated as a proof of trust). Although the model was working, we found that it was structurally unsustainable unless we constantly refinanced, which was a feasible option, but not a very attractive one.

Our features-based approach was a sound way to grow the business by adding value to customers through taking the opportunities offered by new technologies as they became available. We also had a solid lean start-up style methodology, first building a minimum viable product and then iterating until the feature could be delivered to customers. But we'd also hit features' inherent limits to growth – and potential for failure, if we couldn't find our way around them.

In the thick of it, it was hard to figure it out, and adding feature after feature had several structural drawbacks:

1. A feature addresses a market segment, not individual customers. New features, such as refurbished cars, home delivery, etc., did add functionality that spoke to new segments of the population – but in no way guaranteed that we performed our service well for individual customers. On the downside, each attractive new feature added complexity and made it operationally difficult to satisfy customers completely on the one thing that each of them cared most about.

2. The systems needed to support features lead to functional silos and departmental specialization. Every new feature requires internal systems to support it. In the early days, we structured the company around functional departments: sales, IT, logistics, customer service, data analysis, HR, etc. As the company grew and new features were added, requiring more systems development to support them, silos became a reality. Each department increasingly focused on its own job rather than the chain of value needed to perform for customers. Each department started scheduling projects according to its own priorities, becoming swamped with work and late for everything, and engaging with other departments as adversaries more than colleagues.

3. Functional silos accrue power to the top and change internal people dynamics from competence to compliance. As departments took on staff and established their own policies and working culture, power gravitated towards the department heads. Here again, we followed classic business advice and created an "executive committee" to which we delegated operations so that we could focus on more "strategic" thinking. We were slow to realize that our functional heads (without realizing it themselves, probably) soon became overwhelmed with the need to "run" their function – establishing working processes and making them work. This changed our historic "can do" attitude – let's have a crack at it; if it doesn't work first time, let's keep going until it does – to a stodgier "department policy" approach where middle managers increasingly valued people for their loyalty rather than their initiative.

4. As functions establish themselves and build on systems for more features, it's hard to distinguish heritage (we want to keep) from legacy (we want to change). These internal changes, to which we unknowingly contributed and didn't see at the time, contributed to the frustrating feeling that "nothing worked." It wasn't that bad – the company worked, but not well, disappointing both customers and employees. The level of internal friction created by the mix of adding features and projects to get them done to a complex, siloed organization also made it hard to distinguish what was "heritage" (good calls in the past we wanted to protect and continue) from "legacy" (now obsolete ideas that really needed to be changed or evolved). For instance, one of our very early sales practices was "pro and friendly" – our early commercial staff was asked to question constantly what professional and friendly meant in a variety of difficult customer situations. This "pro and friendly" attitude, which we hoped would be part of the DNA of the company, its heritage, disappeared after the first decade without anyone noticing, and we had to rescue it and fight to make it relevant again.

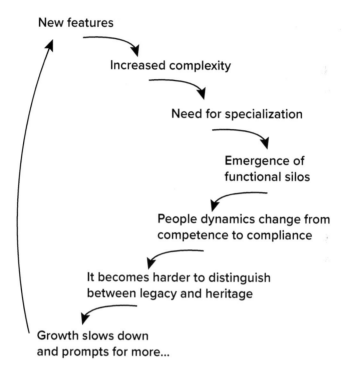

New features

Increased complexity

Need for specialization

Emergence of
functional silos

People dynamics change from
competence to compliance

It becomes harder to distinguish
between legacy and heritage

Growth slows down
and prompts for more...

At the time, it was hard to figure out what was going on – all we saw was one fire burning after another. But with hindsight, we can now see our very growth was the cause of our setbacks. It's not that the promise of digital was not working – it was. It had unexpected consequences that were right in our blind spot because of the very way we'd built the business:

- *We forget that every customer story is unique.* By trying to simplify everything, we often missed out on the unique part of the customer's situation, which we then had to correct for in complicated ways.

- *Functional logic takes over from seeing the overall flow of value to customers.* As operations grew, we could not avoid creating functional poles, whose leaders then saw things from their functional prism and avoided looking at the complexity of delivering value through the entire value stream.

- *People join us for different motivations, and internal growth opportunities narrow.* As we grew into a "normal" company, we had associates in teams doing the work, work for middle managers, and a layer of "decision makers" who were inadvertently dampening internal talent and looking outside for organizational know-how.

- *Legacy and heritage become hard to distinguish.* Many of our early cobbled-together systems had clearly major flaws, and the constant request of our functional leaders was to reinvest to get rid of legacy systems. But we were never sure our older systems did not also hold some heritage – behavior patterns that were key to our early success and that we really should protect rather than get rid of.

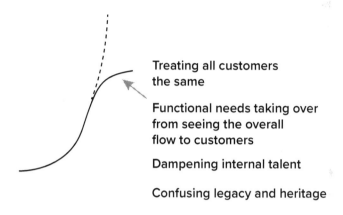

Treating all customers the same

Functional needs taking over from seeing the overall flow to customers

Dampening internal talent

Confusing legacy and heritage

EVERY CUSTOMER STORY IS UNIQUE

Google has the simplest feature ever – a slot for you to fill in your request. But every search is unique. Every customer is looking for a car, but every customer has unique circumstances. For instance, staff have always complained of the peak of customer deliveries on Saturday. Of course, most of our staff work normal business hours. Some customers find it very difficult to get away from work during office hours, so what they're left with to pick up their car is ... Saturday. We've since tried to stay open later on some days of the week, and we have discovered how complicated it was for many customers to come on a Saturday, and simply impossible during office hours. We were then surprised to see how few people showed up throughout the day – rather, we realized, they queued at the opening hours. We are now trying to open earlier on weekdays. Every customer has their own story.

Trying to simplify the purchasing experience is the right thing to do, of course, but simplicity works up to a point – after which it falls over. This is hard to see when you're experiencing it, because the process goes something like this:

1. You offer customers a simple, visible process they are tempted to try. The process works smoothly until it hits a unique circumstance of the customer, a special need, where the customer wants to do things slightly different for reasons of their own (such as picking up the car at 19:00 on a Thursday).

2. Because of the automation, the system is not designed to deal with such requests, and you do what you can to smooth things over and get to the end of the transaction, successfully or not, but the certain outcome is a disgruntled customer (even if they've purchased).

3. When this happens often – as it does when volume increases – you group the top 10 reasons for customer dissatisfaction and build in new features to address them.

4. Each new feature usually involves coding a new system to support it, which increases the complexity of the entire system, which ends up generating an exponential number of bugs you struggle to fix.

5. Because the growing company is incentivized on success (normally so), the process becomes one of selecting the "right" customers (i.e., those that will go through the process without sudden special demands), and discouraging the more complex cases. Growth hides the fact that you are building a stock of detractors who will not only not try your service again, but tell anyone they can it's not worth it.

It took us a long time to grasp the logic of this process, but we were aware of the problem early on because we made a point of listening to every unhappy story from people dealing with our site. From the start, we understood that we live in a wider world than just our website and that our success, in the end, depends on convincing people at large that purchasing cars on the internet is a smart move. Dissatisfied customers might not directly impact our business as we continue to grow (i.e., find more people willing to try), but it's an elephant-in-the-room issue, nonetheless.

Digital offers more autonomy to customers. For argument's sake, let us distinguish between a product and a service:

• *Product:* A product is a thing you buy to do something with. The purpose of a product is to make you more autonomous with it: easier to use, longer lifetime, less need for maintenance. In fact, with decreasing prices, many of us tend to throw away and repurchase products that no longer work perfectly rather than repair them. A product is an object that helps you do something without needing anyone's help.

• *Service:* A service is the help of someone you purchase to get something done. Service involves human assistance. Your car – a product – needs servicing for repair or routine maintenance, at which point you'll deal with people who will do it for you. They will most likely use specialized tools and knowledge that you can't be bothered to acquire.

Many products have evolved from a clever use of technology to replace services. For instance, the capsule coffee machine in your office replaces a trip to the next-door café where someone uses a machine to make and serve you a cup of coffee. Note in passing that convincing people to switch from a service to a product is no easy challenge: to convince people to buy their capsules, Nespresso had to offer the first machines quasi-free, open up luxurious-looking, high-visibility shops, and engage the help of superstar George Clooney and his friends to persuade crowds that making one's own cup of coffee was just as good as having it brought to your table.

The digital revolution we're living through is largely due to the fact that improvements in apps' software have increased a thousandfold the opportunities to turn services into products to make you more autonomous. Need to ask someone something? No need – type your request in Google. Need to talk to your travel agent to book a ticket? No need, use the app. Or to book a hotel? No need either, use the app. And so on.

As you've probably experienced, although it's hugely liberating to buy your travel tickets online, there's always a special case where you need to talk to a person because there's something you don't know how to do and you need the specialized knowledge and tools of another human being – the limit between product and service. This grey area is hugely frustrating because, typically, the site will make it very difficult for you to find where and how to contact support, then put you on hold indefinitely: it is selecting the straightforward customers from the awkward, generating toxic feelings from the rejected ones in the process.

Turning a service into a product means distinguishing the easy, standard use from the tricky, context-specific case. For instance, once you have the technology to make a plug-and-play decent desktop coffee maker, you've made coffee drinkers autonomous. They place a capsule, push the button, and enjoy the coffee. But now they'd like a stronger cup. So you offer a wider variety of coffee capsules. Now they want to drink coffee in the evening, so they want decaffeinated. You offer a decaf line. They like their coffee in a mug. Now the machine has to accommodate different cup sizes. Then a kid scalds themselves playing with the coffee maker. The machines have to be kid-proof. And on it goes. Meanwhile, you have proved that this is a viable market, so competitors move in with a cheaper offer, stealing customers and eating into your margins. Customers demand variety, but not only is variety harder to deliver in the process, it's also more difficult to guarantee the quality of the delivery.

With a greater variety of capsules for sale, it becomes highly likely that someone will want to call you because something went wrong with their order. With volume, the odds increase that the problem has absolutely nothing to do with the coffee machine. The more elaborate the product or its uses, the greater the need of service – having to talk to someone about something. There is a structural trade-off between the simplicity of the product that drives adoption and the added features that give it flexibility but also create complexity. And at some point in the grey area, you hit problems that only a human can solve – no machine has that flexibility, so there's a service-need point, whatever the product.

Concretely, this means that:

1. Customers will always want more: As we offer new products to people, they find new ways to use them or find themselves in new circumstances that can't be done by a machine and need a human to solve the problem.

2. Engineers will always look to automate new features to respond to customer usages and pursue their dream of fully automatic, autonomous products. But as they add new features, they also add exponentially to the complexity of existing systems and increase the likelihood of bugs and failure.

3. Systems will grow in size and complexity as new systems are added to support new features and these systems integrate poorly. Larger, more complex systems are more vulnerable to internal glitches and bugs, they are less flexible, and they make it difficult for staff to go outside the system in order to solve one-off issues for customers.

4. As the overall number of users grows, both the internal costs and the number of dissatisfied users increase as well, creating a drag on the company's growth and sometimes fatally damaging its reputation, particularly if a newer, smarter competitor appears on the scene.

As it scales up, a start-up invariably becomes the victim of its own success. A start-up gets off the ground when enough people find what they offer useful, making the project viable. But then customers ceaselessly invent new configurations that no one had thought about; and, in order to maintain growth, the start-up will respond by adding product features rather than offering service in the form of one-by-one problem-solving. This results in a more complex system where solving each individual problem is actually harder, because it's harder to do something outside of the system.

We went down that road ourselves. We started out with new cars, with a single sales outlet. It was simple, and we focused on solving every customer's specific problems in order to build relationships and reputations. Hard work, but clear.

In 2003, we started adding on sales points. This meant developing a single CRM system that updated in real time for all sales points (we could purchase one cheaply on the market now, but not at the time) and handling multi-outlet deliveries. Our planning and staffing issues exploded exponentially, and productivity fell drastically. Two years later, we started offering financing and upkeep services, seeking both a wider range of customer satisfaction and margins – the car resale margins are razor thin. This meant integrating our partner's tools and processes with our own, and training our staff to a whole new range of products. It also meant much longer interactions with customers, paperwork, and so on, with much back-and-forth.

In 2010, we moved to preowned cars, something we had intended all along. At first, we saw this as purely a good market sense, as the used-car market is about six times larger than the new-vehicle one – but the more we thought about it, the more we realized the immense societal challenge of reducing the pressure on the environment of constant consumption. We saw that a circular economy was a necessary part of solving the problem and that we could contribute significantly by establishing it as a viable consumption solution in the car market.

Here again, complexity increased exponentially. This meant more data fields in every existing system and more features on the website. On top of which, we now had to deal with the logistics of refurbishment and the transformation of our maintenance services. With new cars, the manufacturer handles the warrantee period, and we just managed the interface. With preowned cars, we know how to follow the vehicle over a much longer period of time and deal with the incidents ourselves. Then, logically, we started buybacks, which further increased the complexity of both the site and internal systems, and required new pricing and negotiating skills – as well as making many potential customers upset with the price gap between what they thought they could get for their car and what we could offer (the economics were very different from that in a traditional dealership).

Don't read us wrong – we are convinced that these added features were the right decisions to make and that they both supported our growth and our longer-term vision for our contribution to society. But we were lucid enough to realize that with every added layer of complexity (crossing systems, increasing data fields in systems, adding web features, asking our staff to master more competencies, etc.), we also were increasing our snafu opportunities, which we saw in plummeting customer opinions. We're not a quick repeat business, so churn is hard to evaluate, and it was clear that we were achieving growth the hard way. Indeed, in 2015 it was unclear whether the growth curve was momentarily stalled or whether the tide had turned.

In the fog of war, complexity is not lived as "complexity." Internally it's experienced as conflict and confusion. Conflict because so many new projects now vie for attention and resources. Confusion because everything is important at the same time and the burning fires generated by complexity demand immediate focus while new projects continue to be developed – until they create more fires and so on.

The promise of digital gets you in trouble if you think that *everything* can be automated. The hard part is distinguishing the product and service aspects of what you offer:

• Product consists of the simple, automated features people can use on their own because they correspond to the mainstream case, need to be constantly maintained internally, and are developed for greater security and robustness.

• Service involves staff with problem-solving know-how and latitude in order to help customers with their unique stories and situations. This means creating a culture of people dedicated to fully solving each customer's problem as opposed to redirecting customers to using the automated part of the product – and selecting out all those special cases.

While each customer story is unique, there is a part of this story that is common to all customers and can be simplified and automated. The special circumstances part of the story can be dealt with on a case-by-case basis. Organizations, however, are rarely designed that way, and, more often than not, defending internal processes becomes more important than solving unique customer issues. Creating a customer-focused culture of listening and problem-solving requires, first, realizing how large the problem is, and, second, working hard at it every day.

When the COVID pandemic hit and countries went into lockdown, the auto industry more or less shut itself down. In these early panicky days, we had heated internal debates about compliance, risk, and the cost of remaining open without customers walking through the door. In the end, the lean understanding that every customer story is unique prevailed, and we concluded that as long as some customers needed cars, it was our job to provide them – end of story. Our problem was to set ourselves up to do this safely and (relatively) affordably.

This was absolutely the right call. Our clients then were nurses and firemen – the people who couldn't stay at home in isolation and were needed at work, and so needed to get there, even the more so since many of their usual modes of transport were failing them. Then we also realized that every sales-point story was unique. We didn't issue directions on how to deal with the sanitary situation, but we asked the agency managers to come up with their own plans, to share them amongst themselves, and central was tasked to give them the support they needed. It worked. Although our business fell to less than a third of what it normally was, we continued operating and were lucky to sidestep serious COVID illnesses or local clusters.

What we never saw coming is the incredible surge of business at the end of the lockdown – sales doubled from what they would have been that time the year before. Thankfully, the teams were all on the ball, had continuously organized and reorganized themselves throughout the lockdown, and performed admirably. This was the strangest time for the company, because when all was doom and gloom around us, our teams were full on, taking initiatives, being responsible for their sanitary conditions, and taking care of customers more than ever. In these dire conditions, we pulled through because our managers redoubled efforts to take care of our people. This unusual period illustrated forcefully that our logic should really be:

Individual customer story	>	Local manager and team initiative	>	Central support

And not the usual

Central decision-making and rule	>	Local management compliance	>	One-size-fits-all offer per segment

FUNCTIONAL SILOS WILL DOMINATE THE BUSINESS

We have 30 outlets covering the entire country of France, with additional ones in Spain, Belgium, and now the United Kingdom. Before we knew it, we found ourselves with a sales division, run by a sales VP and so on. When we ventured into used cars, we tried to work with local garages to refurbish the cars we bought for our customers. We quickly grew frustrated with both quality and service, so we decided to launch our own operation and in 2014 created the first refurbishment plant, treating recycling cars as an industrial operation. Now we had a production unit. We have an IT department, a Marketing department, a Logistics department, a Data department, an HR department, a Finance department, even a Look 'n' Feel department. We'd become a normal company.

Organizing by specialty is unavoidable. Even as a start-up, when we were doing everything ourselves, we tended to distribute topics to one or another. The big difference was that we were all working cheek by jowl, sharing the same goals with everyone knowing what everyone else was doing – at a pinch, we could help or replace each other. We knew customers were the life-blood of the company, and we bent over backwards to make it work with every single one. We understood that in order to grow, not only did we need to satisfy every customer, but we also needed to convince the public at large that buying one's car over the internet was a smart move (our marketing slogan was – and is – "How did you buy your car before?").

And boy did we learn! We had endless setbacks, of course, but then we would discuss it amongst ourselves, come up with new ideas to try, and push against con-straints until we found a path to progress. We learned where to source cars. With a hundred years' worth of lobbyism from national automakers, the car business is protected in a hundred different ways in different countries. Europe's official position is that all these regulatory barriers to free movement of goods within the Union should disappear. Within this legal mess, we learned what could be done and what was a real no-

no. We learned to fight legal challenges from dealer networks. We learned to build alliances. We learned to talk to investors. Each learning curve was as steep as the other – as we felt at the time: learn or die.

Ten years into being a successful start-up, things settled down, and we were confronted with a completely different challenge – internal, not external. Internal changes are hard to spot – they just happen. People have clear reasons to alter their behavior, even if they are not good reasons. Everyone defends their immediate reasons for adopting a new stance, which is very different from facing a market change where people blame customers for the change. Yet there is no escaping that both aim and method change when functional silos become dominant. Each functional area develops its own culture independently of the company. Take sales, by example. We were convinced from the start that sales incentives induce strange behavior and detract from what the company aims to do in terms of customer satisfaction. But salespeople expect to work on commission – that's a given to join the company. When we created the sales points, we needed experienced salespeople who could be up to speed quickly with our method. We had to offer them the kind of incentives they recognized and expected.

Each function has its own aims and develops its own methods. Sales culture is all about selling more to maximize one's commission. The sales silo saw our system as a way to convert a customer contact into a sales opportunity. Someone interested in a car model would appear on a sales staff screen as an opportunity to pursue, one that would eventually end up as a sale. Not surprisingly, our best salespeople were not necessarily the best at satisfying customers, but the best at mining the system for the best sales opportunities – customers that seemed like a sure thing. We realized that, of course, and tried to correct it by fiddling with the metrics and incentives, adding complexity and confusion along the way.

The issue is structural and unavoidable. A start-up is made to deliver value to a customer. But as it grows, functions end up seeking to extract profits from customers:

- *Deliver value:* Use your smarts and tech to add value to each step of the process, providing something that customers cannot do on their own and at a price they consider a reasonable value for their money.

• **_Extract profits:_** Maximize the financial incentives you receive from exploiting the resource base you're given.

Any function does that. IT will optimize upgrades while staying within budget. This is what the IT director is incentivized on. She needs to show her boss, her peers, and herself that she has the best IT systems in the business within the budget she's given. Customers are a resource, not a purpose. Customers are selected for pilots, to experiment with new software, etc. Customer satisfaction is monitored to make sure customer complaints (of course everyone always complains about IT) become a visible problem. Customer requests are turned into tickets, which are then planned and acted upon according to availability and so on.

Functions set their own aims and methods and, to carry this through, their own priority and scheduling systems. This is not necessarily a bad thing as these aims, methods, and scheduling systems are the results of decades of experience and should be taken very seriously. Any attempt at sidestepping functional cultures has to be thought through carefully or risk missing out on something in-culture that is necessary or beneficial. But it also means that functions are oriented vertically towards reporting profit towards the top, not horizontally towards helping out final customers.

Specialization is necessary, no argument there. Ask yourself: how many knowledge points (what one has to know to get it right) are needed to succeed at any activity, be it cooking pasta or training an AI algorithm? It makes perfect sense to chunk knowledge into specialized items and to look for the best people within each specialism – no sense in trying to be good at everything. But it has a cost. Two costs, actually. The first obvious cost is coordination. The more specialized the chunks, the greater the need to coordinate all these nodes together to produce a coherent result. But the second cost is deeper and harder to see – the cost of loss of meaning.

Sure, we all need to go to work to bring home a paycheck. Certainly, we look forward to working daily with a friendly group with which we get on well. But what motivates humans more than either money or socializing is *meaning:* seeing that one's work contributes to our team's objective, the company, society as a whole. Meaning comes from agreeing with what we do and how we do it and then seeing it have an impact. The more specialized the task, the harder it is to see how it fits into the overall scheme of things while doing the job, and the harder it is to find work meaningful, which is one of the largest factors of job motivation. As individual meaning is lost, so is collective meaning, and the company as a whole suffers from a loss of focus – which eventually impacts customers as well, creating a vicious circle, as a bad image reflected by customers reinforces the feeling of meaninglessness.

PEOPLE'S MOTIVATIONS CHANGE

The two previous problems of 1) trying to capture new customers by adding features and making the system more complex and less reliable and 2) watching functional logic trump value creation for customers are then compounded as the company grows and people join for changing reasons. When we started, we worked with whoever was crazy enough (or desperate enough) to work with us. Then we started gaining some visibility, and we attracted more highly skilled people with a sense of adventure who wanted to be part of something new. And then we became an established company; we had the pick of top résumés, and we naively started hiring professionals – people who looked to their career first.

Like most founders, we wanted to create a different kind of work environment: somewhere fun and exciting where people could both enjoy themselves at work and realize their ambitions. And as a start-up, this was definitely the case. But then growth started to take a toll, and 10 years later the atmosphere had completely changed. We were seen as tyrannical and respected for our results, but much decried for our management style. We realized this couldn't be good and would not be sustainable, so we asked Brigitte, our first Human Resources manager, to join us; she suggested we participate in the Great Place to Work program. Her skillful touch paid off: we reached 23rd place in the top 50 in 2013, and 25th in 2014, and learned a lot about management. In 2015, we backslid, which showed that few of these changes were deep enough, but we regained ground in 2016 (33rd) and 2017 (17th)[8]. At which point we also realized that, although it had taught us much, the program was making us more of a "normal company": a softer style of command-and-control. On the flip side, we thought we were delegating too much and losing touch with operations, which kept worsening all along. Good management practices were not driving

---

[8] Best Workplaces France, Great Place to Work Institute.
https://www.greatplacetowork.fr/palmares-certifications/tous-nos-palmares/palmares-des-best-workplaces-2017/

us towards excellence, or, indeed, truly unlocking the potential of our people.

Still, we had become a normal company, and we could see we were attracting a different kind of person from the people we had worked with at the start: less prone to try it and see; quicker to defend decisions or processes than try to change them; and, as a whole, more conservative thinkers. We felt we were losing some of our entrepreneurial spirit, both at the front-lines with customer-facing staff and at headquarters, but without quite realizing why. After all, we paid great attention to who we hired and only took the best, or so we thought. We started hiring people from top companies (such as Amazon) and with top-ranked business school degrees.

What was hard to see from the inside was that the company offered very different perspectives for people looking to join us. Our focus had shifted from discovery to delivery. Processes were set up. Jobs were defined. The company was overburdened with headquarters' projects that created endless problems to be solved. We were hiring people to maintain existing processes, not to invent new ways to create value.

Many software-based tech companies dream of a world without management. The idea is that if you organize people in teams and let them get on with it, all will be fine. To some extent, we took that route and hit upon the reality that coordination is absolutely necessary, which means ... middle management. No matter how good the team is, any team will want to focus on doing its job (often as it defines it). The problem is that a team doesn't work alone, but as part of a larger company. In order to let it work, someone has to 1) coordinate with other departments to figure out what the immediate priorities are, 2) share these priorities with the team, and 3) solve the team's workload and morale problems.

In other words, middle managers are faced with an endless flow of problems they can resolve either through *compliance* (complying with the company's processes, systems, regulations, instructions from the top) or through *competence* (using their knowledge and experience to solve problems by getting smart heads together). Faced with the onslaught of difficult situations, middle managers tend to react in one of two ways:

• *Authoritarian:* Managers control the flow of information and impose their solutions to make sure problems are minimized and not seen from above. They reward loyalty and obedience, and punish independent action and, sometimes, even opinions.

• *Problem solver:* Managers take the time to understand issues, debate outcomes with senior leaders and other middle managers, listen to frontline staff, and help them work their way through issues while solving the aspects of the problem that the staff can't access.

One of the ironic difficulties in selecting the right kind of people is that, from the top, authoritarian managers seem the most effective in getting things done or winning internal conflicts (it's not hard to see why they're usually hated by their troops, who rarely speak out of line). Real problem solvers appear as messier, less certain, and often tolerate a much greater level of dissent and confusion in everyday work as they truly work through the issues. Formal evaluation systems are all biased towards smart authoritarians (those who know how not to be too hated), so the path of least resistance is to staff the company with "efficient" middle managers, not realizing you're, in fact, doing the opposite.

Ideally, you're looking for managers with what psychologists call a "growth mindset," rather than a "fixed mindset."[9] This means people who believe that learning is useful, they can learn, and even if the effects are not immediately visible, learning will pay off. They define success in terms of broader (often harder-to-pinpoint) outcomes rather than just defend their narrow outputs and are ready to try new ways and change how they handle things rather than make do with what there is – or worse, jump to red-herring solutions that don't address the real issues but further affirm their authority.

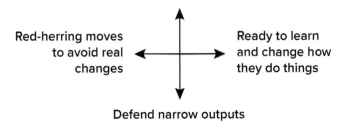

Look to broader outcomes

Red-herring moves to avoid real changes

Ready to learn and change how they do things

Defend narrow outputs

Google's Eric Schmidt points out that behind every real innovation there is a technical engineering insight.[10] To continue to thrive as a company, we need to attract intuitive and inventive engineers – people

[9] C. Dweck (2006). *Mindset*, Ballantine Books, New York.

[10] E. Schmidt & J. Rosenberg (2014). *How Google Works*, John Murray, London.

who take a personal interest in what the company is trying to do and have the space to think and to try things. Creating conditions that compel people to want to work with us and do their jobs well requires encouraging the right kind of managerial culture, which, in turn, means promoting the right kind of managers – never an easy task without a crystal ball.

HERITAGE BECOMES HARD TO TELL APART FROM LEGACY

We discovered that innovation was not just a case of using a new technology to make something work. We also had to solve the problem of *adoption:* by customers, by the market, by our own employees, and by a network of suppliers.

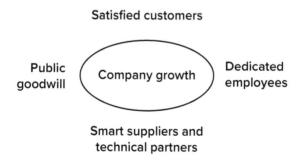

Growing a company in earnest means growing four core assets:

• *A base of satisfied customers:* Satisfied customers are our strongest promoters, period. Satisfying all customers means being able to both deliver our core service flawlessly and efficiently and have the agility to respond case by case to unique customer requests. At first, each customer is a unique event and treated with great care. When you get over 10,000 vehicles sold every year, it's easy to slip into seeing customers as an income to be exploited, no longer an asset to be developed. To grow the asset base of satisfied customers, everyone in the company must retain the spirit that each new customer is our first customer: what did we do to satisfy early customers that we've abandoned?

• *Public goodwill:* The easiest way to gather good press is to propose new features to prospective customers and invest in external marketing and communication. Indeed, we have – rightly – done so. Buy back, satisfied or money back, cars, refurbishment guarantee, financing, home delivery, etc. Yet every new feature that attracts attention is achieved through new projects to develop new systems that increase the internal complexity of running the business and creates a stream of glitches and rigidities that make it hard to fully satisfy existing customers. This, in turn, ramps up the pressure to upgrade all legacy systems and create even more internal projects and confusion.

• *A community of dedicated employees:* Early hires are people we *know* – their ideas, attitudes, and initiatives impact greatly the start-up's trajectory. But as the company grows and defines functions, jobs, and processes, people leave and new employees are increasingly hired to fit the box designed by HR. Leaders are separated from new joiners by both the number of people involved and the layers of management. As an existential asset, people increasingly are seen as human resources to be put to work and no longer individuals to be developed. Yet the future of the company rests on the care each frontline staff offers each new customer and the ingenuity of the solutions each engineer brings to every new technical problem. The community of employees, both in their individual talent and their feeling of shared intention and destiny, is a cornerstone asset for any company, which needs careful development.

• *A network of smart suppliers and technical partners:* Sustaining growth means developing a partner network. In our case, this ranges from sourcing cars to working with government for the paperwork to finding the top technical advice for our leading-edge applications. As you ramp up, you tend to work with whomever you come across, but later on the network of partners can no longer be so haphazard and needs to be seen as an asset to cultivate in order to create space for future growth. Many early practices won't cut it anymore, and attitudes need to change as to how and when to rely on suppliers or contractors to make it work on a longer-term basis.

CHAPTER 3:
PREPARE FOR GROWTH, THEN DECAY

The four key assets – customers, markets, employees, and suppliers – tend to decay as the company grows. There is a structural logic that makes the story unfold in five broad steps – unless you find the appropriate countermeasures to fight gravity. First, you need to understand the problem and the boom-and-bust "iron law" of scale-up.

• *Step one:* The start-up really gets going when somehow it hits a sweet spot where a new idea fits the spirit of the times, and the founders discover the concrete ways to turn one-off events into a regular running business – this is what we did.

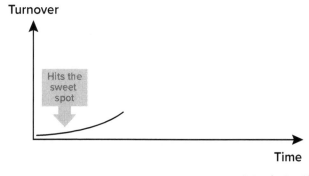

Then there is a period of rapid growth when the general public gets interested and founders scramble to put in place the resources to deliver to rapidly increasing demand.

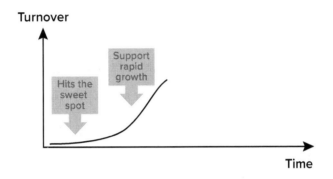

• *Step two:* Rapid growth overburdens internal systems with new features and rigid silos that pursue their own logic. Glitches, bugs, fires, chaos, and conflict turn the company away from satisfying customers and towards fighting internal battles, and, as a consequence, treating customers and staff as resources to be mined rather than assets to be developed. As a result, growth stalls, although no one internally really knows why as everyone is working as hard as ever. Investment in replacing legacy systems by new state-of-the art ones is every functional leader's preferred solution.

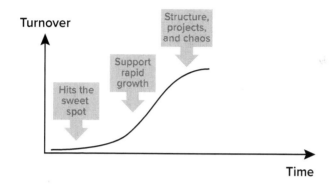

- *Step three:* A chaotic inward-focused situation leads to the promotion of "take charge" leaders who are chosen for their ability to deliver results on outputs and control their processes. As a result, these people do what they know how to do best and increase both the command-and-control of their domains (delivering a stream of reporting profit in the process) and the functional turf wars for resources and blame allocation. Growth continues to slow as customers no longer promote the service as strongly, competitors appear, and new prospects are less tolerant. Investment both in marketing and internal systems now outstrips earnings from profitable operations. Counterintuitively, leaders make the problem worse by hiring managers who do their best to prioritize, organize, staff, and control activities. The business also now draws brutally on scarce resources, such as talented staff, cutting-edge tech partners, and/or willing suppliers, thus creating invisible bottlenecks to growth.

• *Step four:* In 2009, we were flush with funds from a round of financing, and felt overwhelmed by the operations of the company, with fires popping up all over the place. So we did the sensible thing (which everyone encouraged us to do): we recruited experienced hands as CFO, purchasing director, and HR director and then staffed the company with middle managers. In the short term, this seemed to help as we had more people on deck to put out the fires. What it took us a few years to realize is that we had also burdened the company with an added layer of costs and inflexibility as each senior VP brought with them their own work habits and systems. We had asked them to sort the functions out, and they did – their own way. The upshot was stronger silos and greater complexity.

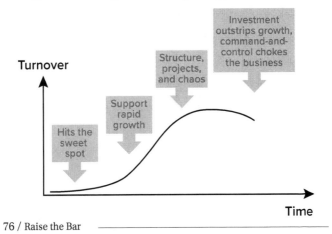

- **Step five:** As sales start to actually drop, cost-effective leaders take control of the business with an armful of solutions to better exploit customers and staff. Although this generates savings on paper, the actual bottom-line and top-line numbers decrease rapidly as leading customers and positive-energy staff desert the company. Compliance and politics trump competence, and harsher and harsher cost-cutting and pie-in-the-sky pivot "remedies" are called for to save what's left of the business.

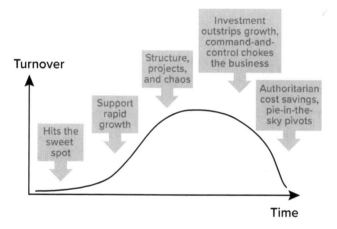

For start-ups that survive, the five steps are likely inevitable. You can, however, turn things around and recapture growth at the moment it starts to slow by changing how you handle the organization and, somehow, as the saying goes, getting the elephant to dance.

We understood well this "iron law" of growth – we'd seen and studied enough companies around us going through the same pattern. We were looking for another response – a different way of handling things.

WHAT GOT YOU HERE WON'T GET YOU THERE

"This is such a waste!" erupted one of our sales associates one day in spring 2012 as we were visiting a branch. "What's the point of trying to do the right thing for the customer if the system won't let you do anything right?" He was right. It was clear that this wasn't working; we had to change something – to take a different approach. We had tried refinancing to launch a new wave of investments in systems upgrades and new functionalities, but matters only seemed to get worse. There was so much chaos and conflict, it was exhausting – and, frankly, not much fun anymore.

To cut to the chase (and spoil the suspense), we did turn around the situation. Having recognized we needed to change our approach to scale up, we decided to adopt a lean approach to growth. We did not know what that meant for a digital business, but Toyota's success in sustaining growth over decades convinced us there must be something to it. And indeed there was.

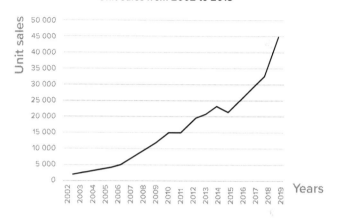

Unit sales from 2002 to 2019

In our digital world, we had seen enough of boom-and-bust (or, more truthfully, boom-bust-refinance-boom-bust) to get seriously worried when we saw our growth slowing and our sales stabilizing. We knew that, one, we would continue to simplify the car purchasing process in order to take pain points away for customers. Two, to do so we would continue to automate as much of the process as we could. Three, we would not give up the advantage of specialist knowledge and functional organization. What we needed to discover was a new way to scale up so that we could manage both the *complexity* of our systems to create more robust products and the *culture* of our outfit to continue to provide top-notch service. We just did not know how.

CHAPTER 4:
GO AND SEE

"I can see your parking lot, but where is your factory?" At the time, we didn't know that "I can see your inventory, but where is your factory?" was the oldest joke in the lean book, and we didn't realize that the sensei was having fun with us, not making fun of us. It was a windy day at the factory, and the wind turbines in the field next door were running full tilt. As we arrived at the plant, rather than go straight to the factory, the sensei had us drive around the lot where our inventory of used cars was parked. It felt silly, driving around all these parked cars, until it dawned on us that, yes, there was *a lot* of inventory sitting there in the wind and dust.

After that first bewildering conversation, we'd decided that the place to start would be our refurbishment factory, which was the closest to an industrial operation and where we thought lean should apply – indeed, we had hired the manager of the facility at the time for his lean experience at an automaker and had received many compliments from outside visitors about our lean process. We were curious to hear what the sensei thought of it. How did we end up driving around in a parking lot being kidded by a lean expert?

We had heard about lean management since business school and had discussed it on and off over the years. We started reading up on it, and "eliminating waste" seemed to fit our problem quite well. We had started to notice more and more crazy stuff that people came up with just to get the job done. For instance, a specific procedure our sales agent was complaining about had been implemented by a financial controller keen to avoid shenanigans and rogue trading – and she was equally upset at everyone complaining about it. At every turn, someone came up with something more to do, with very good reason, but, overall, it just added up into an increasingly unmanageable mess.

We hired Cyril, an experienced lean consultant, to create a lean program, which we called "Haka" to capture the fighting spirit that the *All Blacks* New Zealand rugby team displays in their ceremonial Maori war dance before every game. We found top consultants to coach our team on improvement projects. We gathered from literature that leadership involvement was a key success factor of any lean endeavor, so we had the projects report straight to executive committee level and we took a very personal interest.

Soon we started seeing waste everywhere in the company. This was ironic because our whole business model was built on removing the waste from car purchases: waste of time looking for the right car, waste of negotiating with the dealer, waste of finding the financing, waste of doing the paperwork, etc. And yet, in-house, our very processes were full of waste. For instance, one project succeeded in reducing the time it took us to display a used car on the site from four days to one hour (with a significant cash impact). At one sales point, we reduced nonconformities in part-exchange-cars paperwork from 25% down to 4%. In pilot sites, we also succeeded in halving the delivery time of used cars from 10 days to five – all of these spot results confirmed the improvement potential in the company. The downside of these projects is that the changes never seemed to stick or fix anything beyond the low-hanging fruit.

We knew we had a structural problem of adding too much complexity to the business for what we considered good reasons, such as enhanced customer features or better back-office processes; and we also realized we were doing so by overburdening the business with projects. Our efforts at "lean" had confirmed that a side effect of layering system over system was inefficiency (and disappointed, distressed, and/or disengaged staff) everywhere. But the remedy that consultants recommended was ... more projects, to eliminate the waste that other projects had created. After the initial enthusiasm of the low-hanging fruit gains, our staff started grumbling about the lean projects just as with everything else. A program of lean improvement projects was no path to transformation. Which is how we ended up talking to a "sensei," a veteran of 25 years of lean initiatives, to get a different perspective.

IS THIS NORMAL OR ABNORMAL?

Once we stepped onto the shop floor itself, the sensei pointed to every parked car. "Should it be there?" he would ask. "Is that its normal place? How can we tell?" and "Why is this car not being worked on right now? What's stopping that?" and "What is the quality issue that has pushed this car out of the flow?" and so on. In every case, the factory manager had a very reasonable answer, but as we continued, as in the parking lot, we finally hit upon the fact that there were cars all over the facility, out of the normal process. "Why is this car not at the next step of the process? What went wrong?" the sensei would ask.

Seeing the elephant in the room is never easy when you're not looking straight at it. The plant looked really good – modern, well ordered, clean. We had made a breakthrough innovation by setting up an industrial facility to refurbish preowned cars, and to offer customers a one-year guarantee. At the same time, as we were walking through the plant with the sensei, a TV crew was there to report on how innovative we were, both in applying leading-edge techniques to repairing cars and in our progressive HR policies. We simply couldn't see what was wrong, or what the sensei was pointing at.

Mechanics at a refurbishing bay

To be honest, we thought he was just trying to make the situation look worse than it was to make us pay attention (a classic consulting trick), and we waited to hear how he would handle it, what his solution was – but that never came. He kept asking the same questions again and again.

Over the months and years that followed, as we continued to work together we learned that he was genuinely asking the questions. He wasn't measuring the plant up for a ready-made solution. He was trying to *find* the key problems and figure out what was really going on. As he later told us, he had three questions in his mind:

1. Why wasn't this car at the next step? For every car he saw, whether parked or worked on, he was wondering what stopped it from having moved forward in the process, closer to being driven away by a customer.

2. Why wasn't this person at the next level? For every person he met who explained what they did, he wondered what this person would like to do next and why this hadn't happened yet.

3. How was quality built into the process? What specific knowledge point did each quality mishap reveal, what was the misconception to be cleared, and how to get at it?

His foundational principle was that "to make products, first you need to make people." He believed that the solution to our problems wasn't immediately known or obvious (if not, we would have implemented it ourselves), and would be invented by our staff if we developed them well enough to benefit from their insights, ideas, and initiatives. To his mind, each problem we saw was an opportunity to train someone to better understand how the current process was working and to come up with a better way – hopefully, at some point, stumbling onto truly creative and innovative ideas.

DISCOVERING KNOWLEDGE POINTS

Yes, we agreed that learning was the name of the game. Yet the sensei had a very different understanding of what "learning" meant than we did. For us, "learning" was a rather vague concept, hovering somewhere between finding out new facts, understanding more, and acquiring new skills. Like most people, we felt that one learns from experience – you try stuff; if it works, you do it again and somehow acquire better habits. The sensei saw learning as something more specific. Activities depend on key *knowledge points* (KP). There are things you either 1) know are important, or you don't, and 2) master fully, or you don't. He saw learning in terms of discovering, and then mastering, these knowledge points.

For instance, on that first day looking at all the cars parked within the factory, we did not know the main reason they were not moving was that they were waiting for specific, hard-to-procure parts. In other words, we didn't know to look at every car and ask ourselves "OK, what's the missing part on this one?" We understood it in a general sense, but it could have been something else – no available labor, not scheduled for work, a technical problem that no one knows how to solve, etc. When the teams looked into it and found out about the parts problem, it became a knowledge point: we now know to look at a car as a bunch of critical parts that are hard to procure. Secondly, we didn't know how to master the procurement of these tricky parts. So the teams had to look into it and come up with an array of smart moves to do so, such as identifying reliable sources of certain parts and so on. They learned to master the knowledge point.

A knowledge point is something you have to know in order to succeed at a task: first *know-what*, as in recognize it (it has to come to mind intuitively). Second, *know-how,* the skill to handle it correctly. Learning in that sense is a matter of uncovering the correct KPs (the leverage points that make the difference to performance) and then climbing the learning curve cycle after cycle.

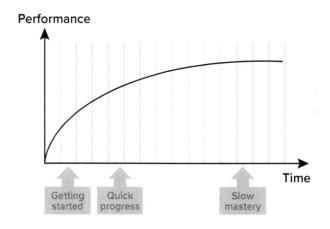

This was the transformation we sought – and it was radical. Rather than invent solutions ourselves or acquire them, we should develop our people so that they took ownership of the problems and found their own answers:

BEFORE	AFTER
Define problems.	Use problems to develop people.
Decide on solutions.	Encourage performance ownership.
Make people apply them.	Support people in discovering their own solutions to typical problems.

The underlying theory is that learning is really familiarization with a problem, not rote application of a solution. Routine solutions are the result of the ongoing process of solving problems and making mistakes. To truly understand the solution, you need to have experienced (or at least understand) the problems it addresses.

On that first visit, we were miles away from that understanding. We were looking for a better mousetrap, expecting a better industrial solution – not a human solution. The sensei was genuine in questioning every car that was not moving. What he was really asking was:

1. What is the unique, specific, concrete problem here?

2. Who should have figured it out if given a chance?

3. How can we build this knowledge into our way of working?

"Why do you want to build a second factory?" the sensei finally asked. "Is it to double your car inventory?" We had shared our plans to build a second facility to keep up with demand. The plant was widely considered a success, and our shareholders were keen on expanding. We felt we'd reached the limits of what could be achieved with this factory, and needed to double our capacity. And, again, at the time we felt he was mocking us. But it was a genuine question – of course the same industrial process would have the same consequences: a second parking lot filled with cars.

This *was* the elephant in the room. We had worked hard at making this factory as efficient as we could, and, to a large extent, succeeded. Starting with a greenfield in 2014, the factory had quickly reached 150 cars per week. But then it could not pass the 200-cars-a-week bar, which we felt was the limit of what it could do. We assumed that the only way to scale up was to invest and replicate our solution – precisely how we had approached scale-up and exactly what we needed to change.

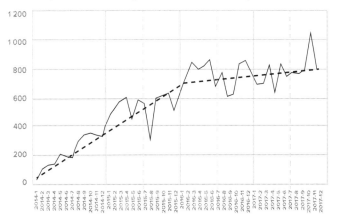

Cars processed monthly at refurbishment facility, 2014 to 2017

"Imagine," he suggested, "that every stationary car in the plant at this present moment is being worked on. How much capacity would you then have?" The answer to that was simple – we would double our throughput right away. That gave us pause. Was he saying there was no need for a second plant?

Okay then. Where should we start? "Let's go back outside," he proposed. "Show me the next cars ready to be shipped on a truck to a sales point." We followed him out, and, of course, we couldn't do that – someone had to look them up on a computer and figure out where they were parked and so on.

According to the sensei, our first step to doubling our throughput should be to paint on the ground a "truck preparation area," a zone where finished cars would be ready to load on trucks. And indeed, as we'd driven in, he had pointed at the mess of waiting trucks on the road outside – which we had explained away as normal because of the day or the hour. How could painting lines on the ground possibly relate to improving throughput? It all sounded too weird for words.

PROBLEMS ARE SINGULAR

When he started repeatedly asking about every car parked within the production hall, as mentioned, one of the production managers realized that a car was taken out of the flow when it was discovered that it needed an unusual part to be fixed or a hard-to-source component. The car was then parked where a space could be found until the component would be procured. Discussing with the parts procurement team, he found that these components were treated as any other parts in the system and would arrive ... when they would arrive. Working with the procurement team leader, they set up a system to prioritize these difficult items and learn how to source them faster. They also made different price/speed calls on the basis that immobilizing the car would be costlier than a minor price difference on the part. To do so, they didn't take a general approach, but looked at each missing part as a singular problem to be solved case by case.

Progressively, the flow in the factory got smoother, and performance stabilized on the higher range of what we thought the plant could do, with promising peaks.

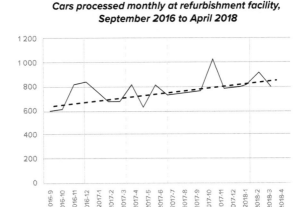

Cars processed monthly at refurbishment facility, September 2016 to April 2018

We believed that if we could process 1,000 cars a month, another facility may not be needed – the capacity was there, somehow. The difficulty was reaching it consistently, but it was promising, and it changed our mind about having reached the throughput limits of the plant.

Fixing the factory is one thing, but how does that relate to our digital scale-up question? When we took the sensei to visit our marketing team, in charge of the website, he asked, "In how many clicks can I buy a car on your site?" The team scoffed at the apparently naïve question. The long and short of it is that you can buy a car directly on the website, but we don't yet know how to handle every purchasing case; so many people choose a car on the site but then purchase at a sales point. Our marketing team had explored this, but the questions stood: Did the site do what it was supposed to do? How well?

"Can you draw the conversation the site has with the customer?" he then asked. "Or conversations?" If our website is supposed to replace talking to a dealer, surely there must be some conversation going on between a customer and the site. Where does that conversation go wrong? As in the plant, the team initially felt that the sensei was trying to put them on the spot and make them look bad in front of their bosses. But no. Here again, the questions were genuine. Before we look for global solutions, we must find our real problems.

Looking at conversations, for instance, our marketing team started with their pitch: the search engine advertising (SEA) they paid for to get the customer's attention. In practice, this means paying Google to show you an ad when you type "car purchase" or to rank your site higher in their responses. In conversation terms, SEA is like saying, "Looking for a car? Look us up." When the team looked into it, it discovered that two-thirds of customers coming from SEA weren't even entering the site. They were blocked from accessing the catalogue if they had not entered their emails and personal details first, which is like a salesperson telling you, "First give me all your details, and then I'll show you what I have on the lot."

Once they started listening, the team heard numerous complaints from customers (too many requests for information), from sales associates (poor quality of leads), and from the marketing team itself (users prevented from browsing the website). Rather than jump to a solution, the team started to unplug the landing pages progressively and check impact. A first 10% of customers were sent to the listing pages rather than the locked landing page. Careful checking showed that these 10% didn't generate less orders than the 90% that went through the details gate. The team then extended the test to 50% of users. The team asked for continuous feedback about the quality of leads from the commercial teams and monitored user complaints. After several months of tracking the changes, they saw a 6% improvement in the conversion rate and a drop in user complaints for those not blocked by the landing page; this convinced the team to drop the gate completely. This had the added benefit of improving our search engine optimization (SEO) - website traffic from non-paid search engine results - as rebound from the site reduced.

As with the factory, the team developed its *problem awareness:*

Take ownership of performance
↘ Find a problem hitherto
unnoticed or untackled
↘ Try and test solutions until
overall performances improve
↘ Discover new knowledge points
in the process
↘ Learn to master the
new knowledge points

As leaders, this is what we wanted, of course. The deeper question was: if they could do it on their own - why hadn't they done so before? The sensei's answer was: because *we* hadn't asked them to.

Again, that gave us pause. Of course, we expected everyone to do their job well. Obviously, customer acquisition was a core mission of our marketing team. What did "we haven't asked them to" mean?

We were beginning to realize that you won't find new solutions in the mindset that created the problem in the first place. As an entrepreneur, you build your company by finding working solutions to generic problems. When the number of our customers increased, for example, we knew we needed an ERP system to be able to follow every customer individually. We could purchase it or build one, a typical make/buy decision. We didn't see anything we really liked in the available commercial solutions at the time, and we had access to relatively cheap and flexible coding resources, so we built one to fit our own specs. It was not the best, nor certainly the most adaptive for future growth, but it did the job. Similarly, as we grew, we needed a network of sales outlets. Same thing – it's not easy, and it's quite a financial and logistical commitment. We found our way to one, then to a second, and established a formula for setting up new sales points, which we replicated to grow the network.

In our experience, scalability was about investing to solve generic problems and then finding the people to work with whatever system we'd invested in. This is how we had built the refurbishment plant. We had tried working with garages and then decided that since we could finance it, we'd be better off with our own factory that we could organize around production line techniques. And it worked – to a point. Because we were always focused on the next generic problem to solve by the best-known solution we could find, we delegated the running of operations to the local managers. We are hands-on managers, and so we never stopped visiting our sites and taking an interest. But when we came across issues, we saw them as generic problems that could be solved centrally with the right pressure point or investment.

For instance, as the number of our customers grew rapidly, we needed to simultaneously better support our customer base while continuing to link cars (wherever they are) with customers (wherever they are), so we interfaced the CRM and ERP systems to get the right car in the right place at the right time at greater volumes. Although obvious on paper, this clever idea generated endless real-world issues with missed deliveries, order cancellations, or purchase-order cancellations – the generic solution seemed smart and unavoidable, but maybe it wasn't. Or take financing. We added the "finance" feature to make it easier for customers rather than requiring them to find financing elsewhere – as well as improve profitability from commissions from our banking partners. As it wasn't our business at all, it seemed obvious to partner with a financing company, as everyone does. This, in turn, became a major headache with difficult interfaces, reworks, reentering information manually, correcting errors and so on. This pattern repeated itself repeatedly. When we started doing buybacks, we went to a smart software solution to calculate our initial bid and then get the price assessed with professional assessors. This created disappointed, cheesed-off customers and exhausted assessors, and was a hardscrabble business.

These generic solutions worked because we made them work. Setting up our own refurbishment facility was clearly the right thing to do. And yet, it came with the headaches of running a plant and the attached supply chain. Generic solutions work – up to a point. To get to the next level in performance, we need to look at problems as singular, not generic. Once we've cracked the main functionality – it sort of, kind of does the job – we need to look at all the small issues, the baby issues, to understand what is really going on and see a path to improved performance.

Back then, we knew all along that our solutions had drawbacks, which is why we looked for software patches. What we didn't realize then was that this made the coder the hero (saving our necks on this one) and the people who did the job the villains (can't they ever get anything right?). In the early days, this wasn't much of a problem because we did everything ourselves hands-on, but as the company grew, we learned to do what they tell you in business school: delegate. Intuitively, we felt, as most bosses do, that the systems were the solution and the people were the problem because they could never adapt as well as we did to specific customer situations.

To tell the truth, we were quite blind to the fact that we were versatile precisely because as founders not only did we understand the business better, but we also ignored the system where and when it suited us – something an operator could never do. Frustration builds on all sides: Managers get upset with staff for not being smarter and more responsive. Staff get upset with their bosses for not being more understanding and helpful. Middle management gets involved and shifts the blame all around. Not good, but this became our business as usual.

Which is why we suspected the sensei of making fun of us when he asked of every car, "Why isn't it at the next step?" or of every customer lead, "Why haven't they purchased a car yet?" or "Why haven't they driven away with it yet?" We thought he was rubbing our noses in a generic problem that we did not know how to solve. What we saw were cars that would be processed and customers who would be served – but not all of them and not all at once. But in fact, the sensei was genuinely curious to understand every *singular* problem. Every car we saw parked in the production hall had a specific reason for being there.

We didn't see the benefit of investigating every specific reason because it seemed unrealistic to find a solution that would take every case into account. Our experience as entrepreneurs is that some losses are a normal cost of doing business and we should not let that slow us, at risk of looking for a perfect answer and never doing anything. But the sensei was not looking for problems he would have to solve. He was looking for problems the people on the ground could solve. He was not *solving* problems, he was *finding* problems.

GO TO THE WORKPLACE TO FIND PROBLEMS, NOT TO FIX THINGS

The first practice of lean, the sensei explained, is *go and see.* Go to the workplace, see what happens, find specific problems, ask people to look into them, and explore solutions ... and the kicker is not necessarily to solve the problem per se, but to understand the problem more deeply. To be honest, this sounded like gobbledygook, but we were willing to give it a go and so we set up the program of workplace visits he'd suggested. What we discovered floored us.

In one of our early visits at a sales point, for instance, we stumbled upon the fact that we asked for a cash deposit of the value of the car at the signature of the contract – quite normally. This amount often exceeded the credit card limits of our customers, and some, who were blocked at that stage, simply gave up on their purchase. To make it easier for customers to purchase, we reduced the deposit to the max limit of credit cards – still a significant sum to deter from defaults, but that wouldn't require the bank's intervention. As a result of this simple change, our sales rose by 3%. Problem solved. Good news, right?

Reducing deposit increases sales

Le changement du processus de commande

Augmentation de 3% des ventes

How could the person in charge of the sales process not have seen that? we wondered. "Did you solve the problem yourself, or did the person who pointed it out solve it?" the sensei asked.

We had to solve it – how could they have? This was a policy that needed changing. In this case, he responded, "Where is the *space for their ideas?*"

Creative ideas are rare, by nature. You don't get creative on demand. You get creative when you obsess about a problem, chew it over, sleep on it, and then one day under the shower – bang! There it is – a different way of attacking the problem. Most of the time we solve known problems with known solutions. The results are, in fact, average, but fine, as long as they're good enough. Why worry about it? On the other hand, superior results come out of building on smarter and smarter ways of doing things. We should be looking for *positive variance*, the smarter way someone has hit upon to do something.

We have been taught that variance in processes was all negative. Shouldn't we have more standardized processes? This assumed that all processes were perfect or perfectly designed – and would be perfect if people only followed them to the letter. But that's plain silly. No two customers have exactly the same demands. No two situations are exactly the same. Problems are an encounter between processes and the reality of context. Variance can be positive if it leads to better outcomes than the current way of doing things. In promoting mindless compliance to processes, we were also forbidding the initiative born from competence.

The difficulty as a boss is that creativity often doesn't appear as such. It's rarely neatly packaged as a new idea with proven solutions. Mostly it's messy and weird. We were struggling with that concept when we had the good fortune of talking to another lean sensei, Marc Onetto. Now retired, Marc served as the operations VP who built Amazon's massive logistics on lean principles. He told us about one of his gemba walks.

One day early on when setting up the Amazon warehouses needed to deliver on Jeff Bezos' Prime promise, Marc was encouraging all sites to practice kaizen in order to get teams to address and resolve new issues that would pop up all the time. In one instance, the internal sensei took him to where employees placed products: operators pushed carts loaded with goods and placed them in the right shelves for pickers to later find for customer order fulfillment. They had standardized the number of items per cart, and the sensei showed Marc that some workers were systematically faster than others. Some would be well ahead of the allotted time, while others would always be late – without any apparent reason. They were not walking faster. They didn't have more items to place.

As Marc recalls, the exact source of imbalance was that all the carts had the same number of items, but all items were not equal in the time it took to stow them onto shelves. Small items were easy to stow, but large items were more difficult to stow as there were fewer locations (a.k.a. pigeonholes) big enough for large items. And often those locations were more difficult to reach (either at the top or bottom of the shelves). The knowledgeable operators could immediately spot a good cart (lots of small items) versus a bad cart (lots of large items). The solution was to create equal carts in terms of *time* to stow: large-item carts would have only 20 items, medium-item carts would have 50 items, and small-item carts would have 100 items. "We spent a little more time at the receiving stations," Marc remembers, "in sorting the items by size into three different carts, but gained lots of time in the stowing tasks by becoming predictable." Predictability also allowed operators to detect other defects, such as scanners that did not charge properly. (Marc detected the problem when he went to work on the line to experiment for himself on the new three-cart standard work and to thank the kaizen team who had resolved the predictability issue.)

The story is striking because it captures three important aspects of a positive variance idea. First, it would only occur to someone who does the job every day, time and time again. Amazon's operations VP was the best there is, but he couldn't think of it. Second, when said like this, it doesn't sound like much. The response is typically, "Oh, OK." Third, it doesn't seem like a scalable solution. It's not complete or workable. In this instance, not all carts can be easier, so how can we possibly benefit from the idea? Positive variance generally occurs when someone:

1. Solves a problem no one has noticed
2. with an unattractive solution
3. that is not obviously scalable.

The kaizen idea didn't seem like much at first, but, as Mark explained, it led to a spectacular breakthrough: "Another interesting benefit of this new standard work for stowing is that it later on allowed us to deploy lean automation, replacing people pushing stowing carts by robots, which bring the shelves to the stower rather than the stower walking to the shelf. In the new automated process, the robots bring the shelves to the stowing station. The stower then puts a certain number of items on the shelves, and the robots take the shelf away and put it back in place. If the stowing process had been as imbalanced as it was before, we would have created a complete logjam of robots waiting for slow stowing. But now we knew how to prearrange the items to be stowed so that the stowing time will be predictable and same for all stations. Without having first solved the balancing process, automating an unpredictable process would have only resulted in total confusion."

At the start of our venture, we had formed our own fair share of quick-and-dirty answers to problems people wouldn't consider, and many of our ugly-duckling solutions had turned into swans as we worked at them. We could well understand how that could happen, but we had not considered it across the company. As the organization grew, unsanctioned patches to system problems had become increasingly frowned upon and were seen as the source of future problems and not as opportunities for creative problem-solving – not without reason, as many fires originated with a forgotten patch no one had fully followed up on.

Marc's deeper lesson that also resonated with us was to separate the predictable from the unpredictable part of every job. Automate the predictable part, then work with the people to find ways to make the unpredictable more predictable. Try it, test it, and then progressively continue to automate. Do not, however, attempt to automate what is unpredictable, or the result will be a costly mess – something that spoke well to our experience.

The radical change of mind for us was that rather than solve all problems ourselves or with our direct reports and then force compliance with our solutions, we needed somehow to create the conditions for *problem awareness:* encouraging people to find problems and test solutions by themselves in order to, later on, standardize or automate them.

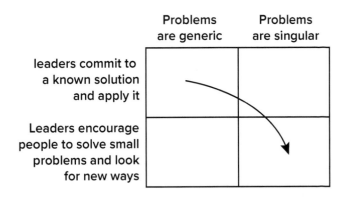

As our sensei had shown, the first step was to commit to regularly "go and see" at every workplace and find problems for people to work on – without taking them on ourselves. This was happening at the plant. We hadn't thought of looking at missing parts item by item, and the plant was taking this on all on its own. It was also a clear illustration of Marc's lesson on distinguishing predictable from unpredictable and then making the unpredictable more predictable by learning about it. The factory's procurement team was learning a lot about part types, provenance, suppliers, and how to handle one case by case.

FROM PROCESSES TO KNOWLEDGE POINTS

Positive variance is only useful as much as it is turned into a knowledge point. As anyone who's practiced a sport knows, the process, the sequence of steps to perform a play, is not enough to succeed. You also need to know 1) what to pay attention to and 2) how to handle it better and better:

Knowledge point (KP) = attention point + work method

In our business, for example, a knowledge point we discovered is the quality of the photography displayed on the site, particularly for secondhand cars. We invested in skill and equipment to make better photos to display on the site – we had to learn how to grow this knowledge point. It's a platitude to say that your performance depends on how many and how well you master knowledge points, but, in fact, most companies are focused on processes and the set sequence of steps you need to do to get a job done, not what you need to know to succeed at each of these steps.

The fact is that knowledge points are often mysterious – they need to be discovered. You learn from direct experience. To do so, you start with a metric and the KPs you already know. And then you look for problems, with the intent of changing your understanding of existing KPs or discovering new ones. In the production facility, the sensei showed us that steps had been clarified on standard procedures but not the knowledge points.

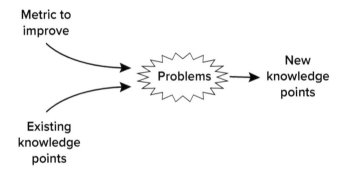

The Amazon placement story stayed with Marc because he was always on the lookout for imbalance (why weren't all performing at the best times) and seeking the knowledge point that would explain that imbalance. Once he found it, through the positive variance he'd noticed, he could run with it. In fact, Marc's story doesn't end there. After Marc had picked up on the positive variance and gotten the team to turn that into a specific knowledge point, he came in to test the new three-cart system. A placer should routinely do the job in 20 minutes, and the team assured him that they did.

Fine, he said, show me a cart and I'll have a go. Nonplussed, the team directed Marc to the first cart on hand, gave him the tablet with the circuit and the flasher to mark where items are placed, and off he went. He returned in double the time. Of course, everyone had fun with it: look, the boss can't do the job properly – what did Amazon's ops VP know about placing products? But then Marc told them he'd struggled with the scanner to flash items. They dismissed it at first, but when they tested the handheld devices, they found that half of them didn't charge properly. There was a problem with the charging setup – they'd discovered a new issue and a potential new, more detailed knowledge point.

Without active problem-finding, new knowledge points can't be found, and performance can't improve. On our own shop floor, for instance, the purchasing team in charge of spare parts to repair cars decided to always pick the supplier with the shortest lead-time in order to accelerate the flow of car repairs. As they did this, they discovered that they made many mistakes when they ordered because they were ordering parts by car model (which sounds sensible enough) and not by chassis type (which was a surprise). Looking at chassis type was a new knowledge point for the team.

We were learning how to go and see, finding singular problems, and viewing what we found through the lens of knowledge points. But to turn this emerging capability into sustainable improvements, we would need everyone everywhere to believe in the approach as we were beginning to. Could that happen?

CHAPTER 5:
INSPIRE A
LEARNING CULTURE

Our early gemba walks were both exciting and frustrating: looking directly to find problems uncovered so many opportunities for quick wins but also progressively gave us a deeper understanding of how our very own policies created the limits to our growth. We were seeing our organization under a different light, and although we had no clue on how to fix it, the potential for growth was definitely there – which was thrilling. Frustrating, because it seemed like we always were the ones to point out problems. People rarely came up to us with a problem that needed fixing or, better, with an idea of how to do so that didn't involve more investment in more systems.

The other brutal discovery from our gemba walk program was the stark difference in how we were welcomed by local managers. Some were keen to have our take on their situation, happy to look into problems and discuss things they could try. They had a "growth mindset," believing that learning was 1) possible and 2) useful. Others were defensive from the get-go and kept touting their results and detailing the long list of reasons things could not be improved (or could, but this would damage something else). They had a "fixed mindset," meaning that they thought that 1) they knew all that is useful to know and 2) looking beyond what they already knew was a waste of time. They both worked equally hard, and the defensive managers often seemed to work even harder at showing that all was under control and nothing more could be achieved.

During our problem-finding expeditions to the workplace, we found out that:

• *The local manager's style creates a local culture.* Growth leaders created cultures where people were approachable, easy to talk to, and forthcoming about both problems and suggestions. With fixed mindset leaders, people would quite visibly dive into their workstation and avoid talking to us as much as they could, staying mum when we tried to engage them in conversations, or occasionally blowing their top when an issue was clearly boiling over, typically looking sideways at their manager rather than talking to us.

- *Local leaders can change their style.* Many who were defensive at first relaxed as they saw us stick with the regular visits. They opened up, seeing that we were expecting exploration, not immediate results. As a result, their teams relaxed as well. Some, of course, never switched to the point that a few left the company altogether. On the other hand, we also saw some growth leaders shut down when they were seriously overburdened either by workload or by a crisis. As they did, so did their teams.

SUPPORT LOCAL LEADERS TO DEVELOP A GROWTH CULTURE

These early gemba walks jolted us and made us change our minds about how we led the business as a whole. Since the beginning, we had been keen to create a different kind of corporate culture, one where people could simultaneously contribute to the business, realize their ambitions, and enjoy themselves at work. Like many CEOs, we believed that HR-driven initiatives and relaxed working conditions were the main levers to affect the culture. We had a "hero" program to communicate internally on how proud we were of our employees. We were convinced we needed to grow trust, camaraderie, and pride in the work we were doing.

But at the same time, we realized that the many work issues people encountered on a daily basis made that difficult, so we tasked HR to find ways to compensate for genuinely difficult jobs.

We had not realized how much our global culture depended on our local leaders. But, in fact, we already knew it. We knew that our sales outlets varied greatly from another. We knew that both atmosphere and results changed when the local team leader changed. But we somehow hadn't grasped the full generality of these experiences. Going regularly to the workplace and seeing local leaders interact with their teams in varying conditions of market, mood, season, events, etc. opened our eyes to how much of the culture was driven by the local leader's orientation rather than by corporate.

As you grow, bureaucratic thinking takes hold. You no longer are focused on finding the right people with the entrepreneurial spirit to get things done, take risks, and learn lessons. You now have an organizational chart with highly specific roles to fill, and staffing soon becomes a numbers game: it doesn't matter who you hire as long as the position is filled. Spending time on the workplace reminded us just how much each individual really mattered, how their outlook, personality, attitude, and experienced influenced everyone else – and the outcomes.

We could see this very clearly in the sales outlets – every manager change is a gamble. For instance, when one of our promising young managers, Antoine, took over from his predecessor, sales increased visibly. We then discovered that the previous manager, without being actually ever wrong, established the wrong culture in small ways: e.g., arranging work hours in a way that he found convenient or worked best for only his staff, helping himself to the fuel intended for customer cars, and demotivating the outlet's star salesman through microhumiliations, with the mistaken belief this would spur him on. When the new manager came in, he repaired the team mood and retained staff that was looking for outside opportunities – the attitude change was visible right away. Unfortunately, we hadn't realized how bad things had gotten; authoritarians often excel at hiding things.

In turn, much of the local leader's orientation was driven by our own demonstration of what we approved of and what we frowned upon. It was painful to admit, but as growth stalled and we got snowed under internal issues, we had unknowingly promoted control-type managers who behaved as if everything was OK-ish and that everyone was working very hard. We were slowly instigating a fixed mindset culture exclusively focused on delivery and with no room for discovery.

In the past, we used to go to the workplace frequently to either audit results or check how someone was doing with this or that crisis. With our gemba walks program, we let the management line deal with results and put out fires - no need to do their job in their stead. We went to the workplace to find problems - look at issues at the source, listen to how people saw things, and encourage them to try things on their own. When something seemed off, we discussed it with the area director to hear their perspective as well. The focus of the workplace visits was *approval of discovery*. We went there specifically to find teams that revealed problems, tackled them on their own, and shared their difficulties. We went to support them in their learning - which also meant reassuring them that learning was not only possible and useful, but a key success factor for the company as a whole. After all, this is how we had originally grown the business.

This shift in attitude changed what we were looking for in a team leader, enabling them to show themselves under a different light. This, in turn, had a surprisingly fast effect on the mood of our people as a whole.

CEO goes to find problems at the workplace and looks for growth mindset local leaders

Local leaders are encouraged that learning is possible, useful, and valued, and many adopt a growth mindset

Company culture change

Team by team atmosphere changes as teams take more of an interest in their work, try their hand at problem-solving, and come up with creative ideas

The importance of local team leaders on the company's culture cannot be stressed enough. Certainly, senior leaders matter. They make decisions, and they set the tone for their chain of command. But culture really happens at the frontline and is driven by these team leaders. As we scaled up, we had let the company pull us in a culture of delivery and nothing else. By going to the workplace directly, we could intervene and try to bring back a balance between discovery and delivery, thus empowering growth-mindset local leaders and visibly changing the culture in a relatively short time. This change was noticeable enough to come up in the press. In one article, the journalist interviewed team leaders describing the change: "In the old days, management came to inspect and point out everything that was wrong," said an outlet manager. "Now they come regularly to observe our working conditions and inquire into concrete, daily difficulties."

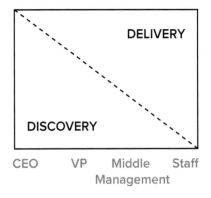

Team leaders also described mistakes made by themselves or their staff to which the management's reaction was "welcome problems" – let's figure out what went wrong and fix it, rather than whose fault it is and who gets the blame. This attitude change was very quickly perceived by our employees and contributed to developing trust in the company and its management.[11]

---

[11] L. Zohin (June 3, 2019). "Aramisauto mise sur le 'comment' plutôt que sur les résultats," *Entreprises et Carrières.*

Discovery needs to happen at two opposite levels to keep the company sharp and competitive: 1) At a strategic level, are we solving the right problems? Are we facing the right challenges? Market conditions keep changing, and generals have a habit of refighting the previous war and missing the point of the current one – so we need to discover continuously what the current challenge of "now!" market conditions are. 2) At a detailed work level, no process is ever perfect, so we need to discover how to make work more effective in terms of higher quality and easier to do (and at a lower cost). Discovery at work level happens through kaizen: small step-by-step improvements tried by the employees themselves in the daily course of their work.

The structural difficulty with delivery is that our minds are designed to reduce complex problems to the part we feel we can solve, or control. It's a feature, not a bug. As a result:

• *Challenges:* Senior executives express challenges in terms of looking for better solutions to problems they already know or, worse, looking for new applications of the solutions they master. The discovery difficulty is facing unfamiliar challenges, such as demographic, sociopolitical, or technologic market changes that change everything and make your current solutions obsolete. The pressure to deliver value in terms of short-term share price increases this tendency to the point that many companies shun any exploration other than short-term tactics.

- *Kaizen:* Frontline employees are under constant pressure to deliver more, and although they think that kaizen is a great idea to reduce the real time spent on work, they also feel they'll get to it after the rest of the To Do list has been achieved. The main discovery problem at the work level is to learn to do the kaizen first – set time aside for kaizen to challenge existing processes and explore new ways of doing things – accepting that not every attempt will be successful, but that there will be learning in every trial, even unsuccessful ones.

As companies scale up, the implicit pressure to deliver becomes relentless. This is unavoidable. What we've learned is that: 1) mid-term ability to deliver in changing market conditions effectively rests on today's space for discovery, and 2) only very senior executives can fight that and create the space needed for discovery by spending time with customers and at the workplace, both internally and with partners; asking discovery questions; using the weight of their seniority to lead by example; and making sure the discovery topics will be followed up seriously by the teams until they find something new.

VISUALIZE PROCESS GAPS TO CREATE LEARNING OPPORTUNITIES

The team leader's attitude to learning greatly impacted the team's ability to solve problems – that was an exciting discovery. But we remained frustrated because we felt that we had to point problems out for the teams to see them (some would acknowledge the problem; some would defend it was not a problem). Why wouldn't people find problems on their own? What couldn't they see? As the sensei told us, what weren't we asking?

Growing up in a digital culture, we had already made visible performance indicators for most teams. Google started a trend in setting up Objectives and Key Results (OKR)[12], and we enthusiastically deployed them throughout the company. Our managers adopted the practice, creating visual boards, whether mark-

---

[12] "Goal Setting," *re:Work*.
https://rework.withgoogle.com/guides/set-goals-with-okrs/steps/introduction/

er-and-whiteboard or digital screens to track a few indicators as close to real time as possible. The theory is that because these goals are mid- to long-term, they are hardly actionable at frontline levels. These goals are expressed as key objectives. For instance, our customer satisfaction goal is expressed as a Net Promoter Score for each sales point, our growth strategy is expressed as monthly sales for each sales point, etc.

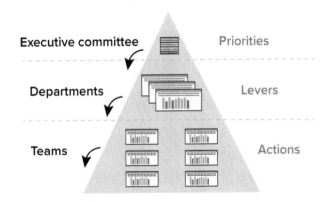

Original Objectives and Key Results (OKR)

These goals drive initiatives and then tasks to be done, action plans, etc. This should allow employees to understand what the company is trying to do and contribute at their level.

The reality we saw at the workplace is that managers tracked a large number of numbers, explained the ups and downs to staff, but had few initiatives other than "work harder" at what they already did. As bosses, our natural response when someone was not meeting their objectives was to ask for more initiatives: What do you intend to do? What do you need to get it done?

"What is the problem you're trying to solve?" was the sensei's starting point. People rarely expected such a direct question, and, when they fumbled their response, the sensei would say to start by visualizing your process. For instance, right from the start as we wanted to improve the on-time delivery from our factory, the sensei suggested we draw squares on the ground to place in advance of each truckload of cars. Here, again, we misunderstood – the sensei was not solving the performance problem. He was trying to find the process problems by making the situation visible.

He was constantly looking for things we couldn't see physically: results. To him, processes came down to results and the activities to achieve these results. A problem was therefore anything that interfered with the activity and lowered the results.

Make processes visible
to reveal problems

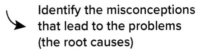 Identify the misconceptions
that lead to the problems
(the root causes)

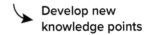 Develop new
knowledge points

From a lean perspective, performance is both a results and a process issue (in the sense of managing the right KPs). A problem is a results performance gap, explained by a process performance gap, and can be explored by asking: what aren't we doing well enough that makes us not hit the target? Asking people to narrow down results performance issues and then take initiative puts pressure on them but doesn't actually help them in any way because they don't see *where* they should intervene. As solutions rarely come out of the mindsets that created the problem in the first place, all too often the initiatives they come up with feed the conditions that reinforce the problem rather than resolve it.

Problem

Target performance

Expected process

Gap

Gap

Real performance

Real-life events

One core lean practice is to physically visualize the tasks that must succeed in order to achieve the result, in such a way that process gaps become clearly visible. For instance, if we want our sales point to receive cars on time to hand them over to their customers at the appointed time, each truck needs to leave exactly on time to start with. Back to Marc's lesson: traffic is unpredictable, but truck departure time should be predictable. For the truck to leave on time, the correct cars should be all lined up ready to load when the truck arrives. Two things we can visualize are therefore:

• Truck loading location and departure time

• Truck preparation emplacement and end-of-preparation time.

Truck preparation area

In order to improve their overarching goal of better delivery, site staff must learn to master two clear goalposts, every day, several times a day: truck departure time and truck preparation time.

Because problems are singular, from one truck to the next, different things will stop the departure of the truck exactly on time, mostly things no one had thought through beforehand (such as the fact that too many trucks arrive at the same time, so the truck can't move into the loading zone). The only practical way to improve this performance is to ask the team to:

1. Notice the first thing that happens that creates a performance loss, and ask, "why?"

2. Try one thing, then the next, then the next.

This process should be repeated until the team progressively discovers the true knowledge points that need to be mastered. But, in order to do this, the visual task to perform must be both intuitive and obvious. Like in sports, you need to get better at shooting the ball into the goal or into the hoop. The target zone can be grasped at first sight as can what needs to be done, which reveals the first cause for performance loss – why did we miss?

We find problems at the workplace others don't see because having built the business from scratch we have a good intuitive grasp of the knowledge points needed to succeed. But as we visit workplace after workplace, we can see that most of the time these knowledge points are very unclear to those doing the work. In a sales point, for instance, we know that the customers' opinion is anchored by their first impression in the first 20 seconds. Yet, so often, as team members are busy with other tasks, customers are left to themselves as they walk in or are asked to wait before being passed on to someone else and so on. First impressions are not definitive, but they count disproportionately, particularly when the person is stressed or ill at ease. And yet, most our team members seemed unaware of this.

This insight was hammered in when, out of curiosity, we visited a nearby Toyota factory. If you picture yourself working on a Toyota line, wherever you are in the factory you can clearly see:

1. The output target to achieve

2. Visible markers of the process steps to perform

3. An alarm or signaling system when something goes wrong on one of these steps

Final inspection at Toyota factory [13]

[13] E. C. Arnold (June 12, 2020). "Toyota Onnaing: why the northern plant was chosen for a major investment," *France Info.*
https://france3-regions.francetvinfo.fr/hauts-de-france/toyota-onnaing-pour-quoi-usine-nordiste-ete-choisie-investissement-taille-1405951.html

Strikingly, we saw their *andon* mechanism: a cord that runs on the side of the line that operators pull when they have a doubt about quality or feel they're late on the pace. This lights up a board showing which station is querying, and the team leader jumps in to help. The matter is either resolved in less than a minute, with the team leader showing the operator how to resolve the issue, lending a hand, and then pulling the cord again to let production continue. Or it can't be resolved in less than a minute, and the line will stop – management comes running, and together they figure out how to correct the problem.

When we discussed this with the facility's management, they emphasized that up to general manager, the primary responsibility of the hierarchy was to make sure visualization and "standard work" was maintained *in order to sustain creative ideas and suggestions.* This involves, for instance, frontline management level (which they call group leader) activities to develop "awareness-eye" and to lead problem-solving.

If we compare, we had many OKRs that needed to be followed and no clear knowledge points to succeed at any one of them. In contrast, Toyota had one or two targets visible in real time and a systematic visualization of each KP to achieve the target.

ROOTING OUT MISCONCEPTIONS

As digital natives, we had accepted that our systems are fundamentally opaque. You type your question in a box, and then the answer comes back, without any insight into how the answering process works. Trust the machine. Our understanding of the workplace visual environment was that it should be pleasant and friendly. Seeing how much the way people present information influences how they think about it was a surprise. We started asking teams to write on their walls:

- Daily objectives and priorities
- Problem analysis

From this we discovered how many implicit assumptions we made about how people understood the business – and how divergent their understanding was. Case by case, we started getting a feeling for Toyota's unique insight that *how people think about what they do* significantly influences global performance.

Toyota's whole outlook is centered on the idea that these misconceptions are costly. Every company making things has a core of fixed costs: wages, rents, and so forth. Toyota's early leaders obsessed with ways to reduce the layer of costs generated by *wrong thinking* in operational methods, such as accepting defects in delivery or holding excessive inventories by producing in big batches. Eliminating these costs contributes to creating competitive advantage and is done through continuous waste elimination and *changing the thinking* that created them in the first place.

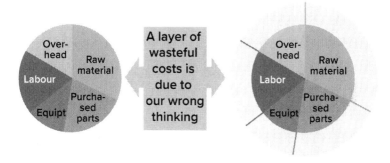

Waste, Toyota leaders saw, is inherent in any process but not unavoidable. *Waste is the result of someone's misconception.* "Lean" is a method dedicated to the total elimination of waste – a method our society badly needs right now – but waste is only the symptom that leads to understanding deeper syndromes (ideas that are considered natural, right and fair, but are in fact wrong) through investigation of the causes of waste.

The greatest impediment to lean thinking is our unshakable belief that there is a normal cost of doing business, always. You can't please all customers. You can't get every part right. You can't always deliver on time. Toyota's unique culture stems from the certainty that there is no such thing as a normal cost. Every activity is seen as a prune with a nut in it – waste is the flesh to be stripped out to get closer to the nut. And the cause of waste is our wrong-headed notions about how things work. Our feeling that we can do without specific knowledge points, that we'll get by.

For instance, our digital model is based on the notion of "customer acquisition." The idea, common in the digital world, is that an "acquired" online customer becomes a "sales opportunity": a name with an email address and a phone number, which can then be cold-called to pursue an opportunity. The rationale is that if people are leaving their details on the site, they are actively looking for something. The instruction to our marketing team was to maximize opportunities, which they did by designing landing pages to push customers to leave their contact details. When a customer landed on one of our pages, they had to enter their information to go further on the site.

This misconception created untold waste for years. Our commercial staff kept calling customers who had no immediate need and didn't want to be sold to, but had left their contact details because the site forced them to – they were mostly browsing or looking at cars. Imagine a shop that asks you for your phone number to let you in to look at the merchandise. Not surprisingly, many phone numbers or emails were bogus, which created further waste of data management. We also lost people who were simply browsing, who didn't want to leave their details and so never went further on the site – and who might have been interested by one of our offers.

We had always thought that getting info upfront from customers was a "normal" cost of doing business on the internet. For years, our marketing strategies were based on thought experiments and best practices in the field, until, finally, Guillaume, our head of marketing, took the initiative to look for waste. He started by collecting every touchpoint with customers through a datalake (a large-scale data storage capability without the constraints of a traditional database) and testing hypotheses about customer journeys through our sites, thus discovering many wrong ideas that led to marketing waste. There is no such thing as a normal cost of doing business.

Taiichi Ohno, the inventor of kanban at Toyota and one of the legendary founders of lean, explained: "There is a secret to the shopfloor just as there is a secret to a magic trick. Let me tell you what it is. To get rid of waste you have to cultivate the ability to see waste. And you have to think about how to get rid of the waste you've seen. You just repeat this – always, everywhere, tirelessly, and relentlessly." [14]

By seeing the waste of having cars parked all around in the plant, we realized the misconception that cars could be pushed through production without making sure parts were supplied first. Then by looking at cars waiting to be fixed in the sales outlet parking lots, we realized the misconception that outlet staff would be diligent about fixing cars because they needed to sell them – truth is, they didn't know how to fix most cars, and didn't have a competent garage around – which was our main reason to set up a production plant in the first place. Forcing yourself to see the waste and ask "why?" you uncover the wrong-headed thinking that led to that waste and truly learn something.

[14] S. Hino (2005). *Inside the Mind of Toyota*, Productivity Press, New York.

We had always intuitively known that people's mistakes were costing money. But we had never seen so clearly how that could be turned into a complete approach to growing a business. By tirelessly solving problems on the shop floor, we could improve the thinking of every individual contributor, day after day, leading to a direct impact on the company's performance.

VISUALIZATION CHANGES THE CULTURE

Toyota sensei insist that you should learn to "look with your feet and think with your hands." The discovery of misconceptions happens at the gemba by "talking to parts, not people" and by switching on the seeing part of the brain, not the talking, discursive part that explains everything as normal. Visualization of the workplace is the entry ticket to lean thinking because it allows people to, in Ohno's terms, understand and agree – and so become persuaded to act together:

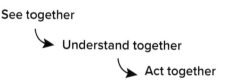

See together
      ↘ Understand together
            ↘ Act together

For this to work, visual signals must be both clear and intuitive. Over the years, Toyota has developed a mastery in visualizing its operations. Early in 2018, we visited a Toyota plant and were struck by the wall-to-wall visualization of:

- **Work areas with physical lines drawn** guide the eye in seeing what is at its right place and what is not.
- **Progress boards** show whether we're progressing on target or not.
- **Alarms** call attention to problems.
- **Standards** clearly and visually explain the sequence of steps to do a task and the knowledge points to master at each step.
- **Reasoning** presents problem analysis and explanation of action proposals.

Toyota's breakthrough is understanding that visualization is the key to 1) noticing problems and 2) getting consensus on the nature of the problem in order to move people to action together. They see what needs to be corrected, and they negotiate the problem-solving process with a common understanding and aim for insight.

It's hard to convince people that such an apparently simple trick could have huge impacts. We were about to learn, however, the power of finding and displaying KPs when, mid-2018, the plant manager left us and his second in command, Rémi, took over.

At first, Rémi didn't quite see why visualizing every single spot of the plant would matter, nor how treating each issue singularly could possibly make a difference. He had learned through his career and working with his former boss that the most efficient way to manage was to look at the top 20% of issues that explained 80% of the variance – the infamous Pareto charts – and they had done well enough so far. But he was curious and open-minded, and he was willing to try. Rémi embarked on a project of visualizing each step of his process. The results were astonishing.

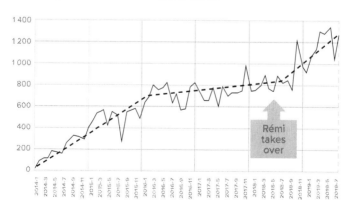

Vehicles per month

No investment was made in the factory. No reorganization. The change was cultural. Rémi moved his teams from the fixed mindset they'd been steeped in to the growth mindset through systematic problem-finding. As they did so, they uncovered problem after problem, solved it, learned, and increased throughput unbelievably – making the discussion about a second facility moot.

KEEP LOOKING

Problem-finding is nothing more than a device to discover knowledge points and achieve higher performance. Visualization is the entry ticket to finding problems. As it's a discovery process, it doesn't always pay off. For instance, when we started investigating the lead-time losses in the production process, the sensei had us visualize the use of our paint booth by breaking down, minute by minute, whether the booth was in use, being prepared for the next car, stopped for lack of work, stopped for a maintenance problem, stopped for lack of materials, something else. The plant manager had suggested the booth was a bottleneck, so the sensei asked us to test the hypothesis.

Visualizing lead-time losses
in the production process

It turned out that the paint booth was not a bottleneck, and, although its use could be optimized, we dropped the monitoring and moved on, looking for a more promising lead. In this case, we learned nothing much about the paint booth. Visualization is not magic – it's the starting point of the enquiry process, not the end point. Discovery means that sometimes you don't find what you expected – which is learning as well. A recurring difficulty with middle management is to persuade very busy people that they should invest time in looking into problems without any guarantee that this will pay back immediately. You don't know beforehand where the key knowledge points are, so the only thing to do is look for them. Sometimes you find them; sometimes you don't – and the difficulty is to motivate people to keep looking.

PERFORMANCE OWNERSHIP

A pilot friend tells us there are two ways to fly a modern plane: *manage the on-board systems* or *fly the plane.* The various monitors, systems, and standards are made to help you fly the plane. They visualize the steady state and tell you there is no problem or that there is one – and where to start to solve it. But there also is the matter of flying the plane as one rides a bicycle or drives a car. Airplanes are now so automated that there is very little flying involved, and some pilots drift into systems administration – they lose their passion for *flying.*

Similarly, modern businesses are scaled up as systems to be monitored, fixed, and upgraded. There are standard processes to do everything, but few real knowledge points. Increasingly, the risk is that everyone loses the physical, emotional, and intellectual sense of growing the business.

Visualization – the art of defining "strike zones" and looking for knowledge points – is a hard skill to learn. As we carried on with our program of workplace visits, we were struck by the fact that we met many resources or process owners – but who owned *performance?* It was easy to see it in the factory. We're a digital company. We've got screens monitoring actual versus target everywhere, with lots of green and red numbers. But when we asked for the key performance at first to drive the business, we got ... no answer. To us, it seemed obvious that the one thing that mattered was a greater throughput of quality cars to satisfy the growing demand of our secondhand business. To the plant's management team, it was unclear – they had so many indicators to get right. What struck us with the management system we had put in place is that there were two opposite ways to use it:

• Own the performance that drives the business and use all other indicators as analysis points to uncover problems, solve them, and improve the main thing.

• Monitor and manage all the indicators to keep them at a stable level and then explain away the fact that the key performance itself was not improving.

You can either monitor the systems or fly the plane. It's the same plane, with the same onboard systems.

Factories are concrete. They're easy to figure out when you look hard enough, because you can see most of what goes on. But the further we moved towards digital and software, the worse it got – more indicators, less clarity on performance.

As we've seen, in a digital company, in order to sustain growth, it's tempting to add more services and features to existing systems to try and capture new customers. With lean, we changed our minds and realized what we *had* to scale was smooth and seamless customer interactions. This radical change of perspective made us realize the true difficulty of scaling: scaling systems is a matter of adding work to work – the technical solutions are there, eventually, and the system will handle a higher number of transactions. Scaling customer interactions, however, is a completely different kettle of fish. It's no longer a question of just getting the system to do a job, but one of making sure the system is easy to handle, puts the human using it in a good mood, and is willing to serve rather than just sell. In practice, this meant making everything simpler, not harder for sales outlet staff, which is how we decided to pull cars in the outlets (the day before the appointment) and make sure they would only receive good-to-go cars (reducing progressively the number of "delinquent" cars the agencies received). We needed to reduce problems the agencies faced so they could focus on customers' unique circumstances and requests.

We had been trying to scale technical solutions. The sensei's persistent *problem-finding* at the workplace had shown us that to keep growing the answer was *cultural.* Systems had to work for people, and people had to be intent on solving customer problems in a way that pleased the customer, first, and the company, second. By spending time at the gemba, we saw that we had tried to solve our complexity and bugs situation by adding more projects, processes, and controls, which in effect made the problem worse. We learned that it's pointless to apply solutions unless the problem is well understood. We also learned that we could easily find problems and think of solutions, but it was much harder to get our people to take ownership for performance, find problems themselves, and look for their own solutions. To create a growth culture, we needed to learn how to engage people more systematically in their own problem-finding, problem-solving, and sharing of knowledge points.

CHAPTER 6:
ORIENT AND SUPPORT

The first gemba walk in our data science department didn't go as expected but was somewhat comical in hindsight. We'd gotten used to gemba walks in the plant and in sales outlets, where people had come to better understand problem-solving and were relaxed with the challenging nature of looking for problems. But when we walked into the open space of data science at headquarters, a few heads looked up inquisitively and then promptly dove back into their screens. After a moment of confusion – the manager wasn't on site – a team leader finally walked up to us. He introduced the department, and then the sensei asked him: "Could you list the questions you are currently answering for the business?" The team leader stared back, puzzled. Then: "Would you be able to visualize on the wall your answers to these questions?"

After we'd clarified why the odd questions were being asked, the data team leader explained that this was not how the department worked. They were data specialists. They worked with cutting-edge techniques, such as random forest and other supervised learning approaches, to solve difficult problems, such as pricing, and then plugged the result directly into the system: Users just had to use it. Users didn't have to understand how the calculation worked. Alejandro, the operations VP, who was doing the gemba walk with us, laughed. "I would like to understand the calculations," he said. "How can my teams use the system smartly if they don't get how it works?"

It's astonishing to see how far the legacy of Taylorism reaches in our enterprises: engineers design the process, and frontline grunts apply the process they're given. Wherever we turned, we found the same assumption: fix the digital system, and then get people to comply to it. And the same response: people used systems minimally and in very idiosyncratic ways. In many cases, we found that they bypassed the system altogether and used old-fashioned spreadsheets and such. When asked why, they explained that the issue they were working on couldn't be solved by the system – or, more accurately, that it probably could, but they thought that learning to master the software would take more time than just doing the work directly. When asked how the issue at hand impacted performance, they looked at us like we didn't know anything but were at pains to answer.

Time and time again, the sensei insisted: "What is the gain? What do you seek to improve?" And then he would challenge the logic of the answers: "I don't see how this follows from that." We thought that he was challenging our people's thinking – and that he was a bit harsh about it. Surely, they were doing their best. But just as we had misinterpreted the sensei's earlier problem-finding that put us on the spot and served as a wakeup call, here, too, we didn't understand his intent. He again was genuinely interested in singular problems, but it took us a while to realize the sensei's questions were challenging *motivation* more than reasoning.

Then he addressed us: "Where is the line of sight?" His question sought to understand the clear objective on the horizon, the visible goalpost towards which everyone here should be working – *would be* working if they could see it. How do you orient people so they spontaneously do the right thing for themselves, the customer, and the company?

We had set up a regular calendar of gemba walks on our own and now were becoming familiar with the different welcomes we got from team to team. Some teams jumped right in with the problem-finding, discussed issues, thought aloud what could be done, and committed to an experiment to get started. Other teams stayed sullen and defensive and would not commit to any change. We'd learned to follow up on the former and not get too annoyed at the latter – not easy for us, as some of these conversations could become really frustrating.

Discussing this back and forth, we realized once again that the problem was ... us. We simply assumed that people came to work to solve problems. But this assumption turns out to be really weak. Most people come to work to do a job. They see problems as annoyances, obstacles that get in the way of getting the day done and going home. Problem-solving was not just a question of cognitive capacity, but one of wanting to do so. What did we, as senior leaders, do to engage staff in problem-solving? Not a lot. This was a new challenge altogether. We needed to reframe our gemba walks from audits to see that people were on top of things, to an activity towards creating a culture where problems are welcome and seen as the main source of improvement.

The breakthrough of a lean perspective is to build a problem-solving culture by seeking everyone's voluntary participation to improve quality and reduce lead-time and total cost. *Voluntary* being the crucial word. During the gemba walks, we were interested in problems and immediately looking for solutions – of course, it was vital to us as founders and leaders of the company. But why would it be vital to someone who just worked there? The sensei was not that worried about finding the right solution right away. He knew from experience that when people start digging at a problem, they eventually figure it out and find smart ways to do so. He was interested in the *impulse* that made people interested or not. He was trying to help us understand what prompted voluntary participation to performance as opposed to forced participation to the process because this is just the job.

We're all natural problem solvers. The questions are: which problem and with what solution? We are instinctively prone to move to:

• ***Correct a dissatisfaction:*** More than seek advantage, something that seems "not right" creates a tension to action that motivates us to do something, according to perceived opportunity and clear path.

• *Negotiate a solution:* We are social animals. Few of us are prone to act first and speak later. Mostly, our instinct is to discuss the situation, express our intentions, look for support, and seek a negotiated solution.

• *Monitor a situation:* When we've invested in action and are invested in an outcome, we also do what it takes to keep abreast of the situation and check for positive or negative evolution.[15]

The interesting issue is: which problems?

The lightbulb was turned on one day when we were visiting a distant sales point with the sensei and stopped for a second just as we got out of the car to take a deep breath and look. At that moment, an elderly gentleman parked his car next to ours and climbed out. He then opened the rear door and pulled out a bulky child seat, which he struggled with, carrying it all the way into the branch. As things were set up, the customer entrance was at the end of a long walkway, but there was a side door closer to the parking lot where some of our sales associates were taking a break. They watched impassively as the old gent lugged the seat all the way to the

---

[15] A. Damasio (2018). *The Strange Order of Things: Life, Feelings and the Making of Cultures,* Vintage, New York.

front door. Evidently, we were irritated by the staff's attitude and lack of initiative, but the sensei asked us: "You see a problem: a customer we could have helped better. But what do *they* see? What is their problem?" That was easy. They were on their break, and their problem was taking a breather from work without being interrupted. And if you keep asking "why?" the real problem was the long drive between the parking spot and the branch's entrance – altogether another issue.

This was a rather extreme case of an ordinary situation. In almost every sales point we visit, customers are waiting while staff are busy doing something else. In truth, the same happens in half the restaurants and shops you walk into. We were looking at two very different *views* on problems:

	CUSTOMER	STAFF
Correct a dissatisfaction	Get served now.	Finish the job at hand.
Negotiate a solution	Wait your turn or clamor for attention.	Tell the customer that someone will be there presently.
Monitor the process	Balance the attractiveness of the solution with the release of walking out.	Balance the urgency of finishing your work with the hassle of dealing with an upset customer.

When you walk into one of our branches, you're about to make one of the most expensive purchases of your life (in most cases, the second highest). This is a fairly unique moment that can be both fun and stressful. When our sales assistants see you walk in, they are in fact seeing the 10th person today, on top of all those of yesterday and the day before and so on. Meanwhile, they have their reporting to send to headquarters, their manager has asked them to finish something else, and the network is crashing, so they can't use the computer.

It was quite clear to us that a growth culture rested on the *continuity of customer satisfaction.* Our ideal was to treat each new customer as our first customer, with what we used to call "professional and friendly" service when we started – our first mantra. As we now grasped, the company scale-up invited a fixed culture based on the *defense of the status quo.* Both the motivation and type of problems these two cultures present are quite different:

	GROWTH CULTURE	FIXED CULTURE
Correct a dissatis-faction	Solve all customers' problems completely to make sure they will recommend us to their friends. Make sure all team members feel at ease in their job and in front of customers.	Protect one's comfort zone within the compliance of company's procedures and processes. Make sure no one speaks up or takes unsanctioned initiatives.
Negotiate a solution	Discuss with the team and negotiate with headquarters to find a way to solve problems within the existing systems. Encourage immediate initiative. Share solutions with others to clarify knowledge points.	Defend the process: explain to customers why they can't get what they want, and ask for investment in more and better tools. Enforce compliance to keep everything – and everyone – quiet. Explain away setbacks as unusual circumstances.
Monitor the process	Look at how quickly customers' problems get solved and how open and helpful the problem-solving process is internally, particularly across functional barriers. Look to learn new knowledge points to improve performance.	Always look good and never look bad. Make sure all problems are contained in the area and that blame falls on other departments. Keep track of loyalty and dissent. Audit the compliance to all processes.

In other words, a culture is defined by 1) what type of problems are worth pursuing and what kind are not, 2) what kind of solutions are favored and what kind are not, and 3) what habits are routinely followed and what questions are OK to ask. To support a growth culture, we needed to align everyone on the continuity of customer satisfaction and on solving problems autonomously. We also needed to encourage people to speak up when they saw something not quite right. This, in turn, involved setting up an education system across the company. Not a small task. Where and how should we start?

FACING PROBLEMS

The real problem, according to the sensei, was not just finding problems, but *facing* them. When we were discussing the fact that none of the associates taking a break would get up and go help our customer with his child's seat, we were refusing to face the fact that the entrance was too far. Fixing the team's attitude was more palatable to us than changing the doorway, which would mean refurbishing the whole shop.

When we visit another company, we're always surprised at how management teams can totally ignore the quite obvious elephant in the room. But internally the same always happens. We all naturally and normally decide that too-big problems are off the table as well as small problems without easy solutions, and the social negotiation process then makes sure the question will not be addressed by anyone in the room. Worse, middle management then makes sure that the question won't come up, in defense of the status quo.

"What are the three most important moments for your customers?" the sensei asked. That was easy. Finding a car they liked, paying for it, and then taking delivery. "What are the key performance losses on each one?" Easy as well: sourcing popular models at a good price on the site (if they're popular, it is more difficult for us to negotiate good deals with our suppliers), helping the customer find a model they can afford when it's not the one they first wanted, and delivering the car at the exact appointed time and day. "What are you worst at?" Delivery: our on-time delivery was horrendous, no better than 50%.

Let's start there, then. Face it.

We believed that this was a problem we couldn't solve because we had tried and tried without luck, and it's also common market practice to be late on delivery. In the early days, we would handle the trucks ourselves, and we somehow managed to be agile and reactive. Progressively, as we grew, logistics became a full department, and a caricature of a fixed culture: militant about its processes, inflexible, and a real fortress – no way in. For our initial attempts at fixing the problem, we used "milk runs," which we had learned about when we first looked into lean. This lean logistics concept consists of a fixed route with multiple stops where the truck picks up various parts from each of the suppliers on the stops. It runs on a fixed schedule, with the assumption that all parts the truck is coming to pick up are ready and waiting beforehand for quick loading. We hired an engineer to implement a milk-run solution, and things went from bad to worse. His answer was to implement a new software solution, which we clearly didn't want to do. Our feeling at the time was that our supply chain had become so complex that it was unmanageable. This feeling was validated by visiting digital outfits of large retailers that didn't seem to be doing any better than we were. As for Amazon, we told ourselves they had achieved better results through the sheer weight of their investment.

"Where are the cars you're expecting to deliver to-morrow?" the sensei asked the branch manager. We had heard this before in the refurbishment factory, and we felt the manager's pain when he looked to the parking lot full of cars and indicated they were somewhere in there. "Of all the cars, how many do you expect to hand over to customers tomorrow?" About 10. "Why are the others here then?" Because logistics delivered them. "If you don't need them, why don't you send them back?" The branch manager looked at us in silent entreaty. Of course he couldn't send them back – logistics would never allow that. And if he did, the chances are that he wouldn't have them back when they were needed for customers.

Orienting means literally turning people's attention so that they face the right problem to solve, and, more deeply, the right challenge to respond to. The sensei was trying to move "parking lot full of cars not about to be delivered" from the "normal, not a problem" box to "abnormal, problem to be solved" box. He was trying to help us face the problem. The branch manager, on the other hand, was understandably stressed because: 1) he was not sure it was a *real* problem (although he agreed having to change delivery dates with customers was a real pain point) and couldn't see how having fewer cars on hand would help; 2) he didn't see a path to doing it and probably didn't feel up to it. We not only felt and shared his pain; we saw our role in causing it. We began to understand what the sensei was trying to introduce: the contrast of our traditional "command-and-control" to lean's "orient-and-support."

TRADITIONAL	LEAN
Command: Solve the problem and tell people what to do to apply your solution.	Orient: Make them face the problem by showing it and insisting it needs to be solved.
Control: Check that they're applying instructions and correct when needed.	Support: Give them practical help and approval when they try something.

Stress is not all bad. Some stress is a motivator, the emotion that moves us to correct a dissatisfaction. Too much stress, of course, is harmful – both in the damaging behaviors it induces and its direct impact on our health. There is good stress (eustress) that moves you positively and bad stress (distress) that hurts you. Stress is the result of the gap between the perceived challenge and our perceived ability to handle it. Performance follows a stress curve.

Performance Stress Curve

"What is the difference between distress and eustress"
https://readbiology.com/difference-between-distress-and-eustress/

Facing problems is definitely a stressor. Facing the problems we find is the entry point for learning. But it also needs to be eased into so that people are moved to action rather than discouraged into apathy. To help people face problems, we can intervene in three ways:

1. Welcome problems.
2. Develop autonomy in problem-solving.
3. Help with roadblocks.

BAD NEWS FIRST

"Tell me the bad news first" is one of the precepts we heard the most often from the Toyota veterans we talked to as we delved more deeply into lean. They are convinced that "bad news first" is one of the things that makes Toyota so different from any other company. Their reasoning is that everyone wants to share the good news, but if there is good news, there is nothing to learn. Toyota sees a culture of problem-solving as the key to its success and its adaptability to ever-changing circumstances of the automotive industry – and problem-solving starts with bad news. As they say, "no problem is a problem."

To be honest, we were easy to convince. In the early years, we practiced this by visiting sales points and trying to think of ways to get the teams to do better and deal better with their issues. When we got to the point of having regional directors for our network, each in charge of several sales outlets, their original brief was to come back from every workplace visit with one thing they would do to make their staff's life easier. But with so many other good intentions that worked well at the start, this got lost in the scale-up. With increasingly complex systems, increasingly hard to change, you stop listening to people simply because you no longer know what to tell them – solutions are forever getting harder to find and out of reach of simple actions.

For instance, cars are not delivered on time at the sales point, but no one tells us because it has been accepted as common market practice. Car registration times increase, but, really, it's not our fault that the government makes the procedure increasingly complicated – sales directors tell people to get on with it and stop using that as an excuse not to make their numbers. Cars arrive damaged at the sales outlet: clearly, an outlet manager should know how to find local mechanics to solve such problems. Customers are unhappy to find their order cancelled after 72 hours if it isn't confirmed – so what, stock rotation is a key driver for the company and more important than how some customers feel. You can't please everyone every day. As issues arise like a tennis ball machine spewing problems, it's easy to slip into a fortress mentality and bat every problem aside, accepting all complaints as a normal cost of doing business.

Then the sensei comes along and asks staff to list problems on walls. The initial reaction is close to despair. There is no way we'll ever be able to tackle all of this! As we found out when we tried asking staff for bad news, this goes profoundly against all instincts. No one wants to be the one to tell the boss the wrong thing. Everyone automatically shies from the "shoot the messenger" moment. And, indeed, we've seen it in ourselves and other CEOs we've visited. When told something you don't want to hear, you tend to either dismiss it or argue against it. Sometimes you're right – what they were telling you was nonsense. But often they have something to tell you, and you immediately put up a big "shut up" sign so you'll never know.

"Tell me more?" is a phrase you have to teach yourself to establish a culture of bad news first. When someone has something difficult to report, they will feel defensive and it won't come out right – either too timid or, on the contrary, too brash and provocative. People expect you to react badly, so they brace themselves for the slap. And indeed, anger, numb shock, or disbelief is a normal reaction to bad news. The worse the news, the stronger the reaction. People feel good giving good news, bad giving bad news. Encouraging bad news is a learned skill – one that needs to be practiced time and time again. For instance, at the workplace we had to learn to be very careful with formulating "tell me more" rather than the more instinctual "why didn't you ...?" Employees who speak up run the real risk of being corrected or blamed by their manager who says, "Come on, surely, you should have thought/done/dealt this or that." Or is upset with them because they shared something with the leader the middle manager would rather have kept quiet.

When we are on the gemba and someone comes up with a bad news point, or we challenge them on a problem and they come up with the bad news, *the way we react* either builds the culture of trust and problem-solving by encouraging high-road thinking or, on the contrary, weakens it by triggering low-road, knee-jerk responses. Mimesis, human beings' tendency to reproduce (consciously or unconsciously) their leaders' behavior, remains the strongest management behavioral driver.

This means that spending time at the workplace just to listen to people and have them discuss problems is, in fact, forceful action towards building a growth culture and a very concrete lever to solve our scale-up challenge. As you can imagine, this feels completely counterintuitive. We were taught to be take-charge leaders. To make quick, decisive judgment calls. To command and control by giving clear instructions for others to follow. And, indeed, this is how we built a very successful business. Or so we thought. Talk about bad news first: now we are considering the fact that we built the business in spite of our take-charge attitude. And to be completely honest, when we look back, we can congratulate ourselves on a few good calls, but we also can list all the wrong-headed decisions we took that slowed us down and would have gone completely differently if we'd listened more and supported the people on the ground.

The logistics milk-run project is a point in case. Our objective was to reduce delivery lead-time to 2.5 days as well as achieve 95% on-time delivery (OTD). We could have tackled practical issues people had with the existing system and fixed them one by one, using their initiatives, but, at the time, we went the system way. We looked to upgrade our global logistics system with a new transport scheme with the stated objectives of minimizing transport costs by optimizing truck loads and reducing lead-time by massifying transport: a truck would load cars for several sales outlets and do a "milk run" to deliver the cars by doing rounds in a fixed path to deliver to agencies. There is nothing wrong with the principle on paper, and we'll probably get there in the end, but at the time we didn't listen to frontline operators who argued that the challenge of lead-time and OTD didn't square with the cost reduction and consolidation objectives.

Operationally, the engineers in charge of the project envisioned a digital solution where cars would be scanned with a QR code at every point so that we could calculate the most "efficient" routes – again, something that we're currently in the process of achieving with the pull system, albeit in a very different way. The anticipated benefits of the system were better planning of transports, greater simplicity of the sales outlet network, higher transport productivity, and preparing the company for growth. What the system view ignored was that we didn't master logistics on the ground – neither at handling cars precisely on parks nor at controlling transport at the truck level, which everyone believed was impossible.

As the scheme got underway, we systematically ignored bad news (described as "resistance to change"), and, in the end, the project turned into a full-scale fiasco with the lowest OTD ever. When we tackled the problem again with the sensei, we started by looking at the bad news for every car and building logistics capability from scratch: the know-how to move a car from one specific place to another at a specific time. We scrapped the high-level plan and got everyone involved in the chain to work on single issues, one at a time, starting by visualizing parking spaces and truckloads – all the way to reception at sales point. In the end, we got progressively closer to our objectives, both in terms of lead-time, OTD, and overall costs – not by implementing a new system top-down but by involving every actor in the process in solving practical issues on a daily basis. We certainly could have saved ourselves a lot of pain and unnecessary costs by starting with listening to the bad news.

In the end, we reduced customer wait times for their cars from three or four weeks to 24 hours – a spectacular feat by our logistics team and a decisive competitive advantage. But we got there by orienting to a clear line of sight (reduce customer lead-time) and solving one problem after another, not by implementing a best practice with a road map and action plans.

"Bad news first" is just the tip of the iceberg of the radical leadership pivot from making all the decisions and then finding people to execute them to developing people and then supporting their initiatives. "Bad news first" is the prerequisite attitude to enabling problem awareness – both for ourselves and others. Establishing "bad news first" as a norm is the first step to create a safe environment for problems to be addressed and discussed, so that unfavorable information is shared as well as positive.

A SOURCE OF COMPETITIVE ADVANTAGE

Lean starts at the customer service department, which is an excellent source of bad news. Every customer complaint is 1) a customer we can win back if we handle this correctly, 2) something we can fix in our service to be better than our competitors (if it's hard, they're no more likely than us to get it right), and 3) a potential source of discovery of disruptive innovation. After all, our entire business venture was built on people around us complaining of their car-buying experience at a dealership.

Customer service handled many calls about rescheduling a delivery. A common complaint from customers was queuing on Saturdays when they came to pick up their cars – many customers had other things on their schedule, and when they saw the line, would reschedule the transaction, which created all sorts of havoc both for them and for us. Looking into it, it made sense – our outlets follow normal business hours from 10:00 to 18:00 – but customers work as well, so 18:00 on weekdays doesn't help them much. We worked with outlets to expand opening hours to 19:00 in order to take some of the load off Saturdays.

Improvement opportunities are everywhere. The business has structural issues that are hard to solve. This gives us endless potential to improve the process and come up with creative ideas to serve our customers *on issues that matter to them,* better than the competition can.

We look for opportunities across five dimensions: quality, capacity, flexibility, connectivity, and value for money. True, every businessperson knows that if they improve on all of these, sales should follow. But few know how to do it. Over time, we have changed the way in which we think about each one:

OPPORTUNITY	ISSUE	LEAN APPROACH
Quality	Customers are disappointed by a perceived gap between our promise and our performance and want some value back. We inspect quality at the end of the process but cannot fix all the problems we find.	Building quality in the process means understanding the promise in detail, finding out what needs to be mastered at each step of the process, and then engaging people in checking and improving their own quality.

OPPORTUNITY	ISSUE	LEAN APPROACH
Capacity	In our business, customers will complain that the planned delivery is too late for their need – they need the car to go off on holiday next week. They're not complaining about our service; in fact, they want more of it and faster.	Volume flexibility is a key concern. We need to be able to accelerate or slow the rhythm at which we deliver to customers, and this means knowing how to work with temporary resources.
Flexibility	They want an option we haven't got at hand and don't know how to source easily. We can do it, but not right away because we're busy doing something else.	Small batches and rapid changeovers are the key to being able to shift quickly from one job to the next and offer multiple customers what they want right now.
Connectivity	They complain about a bad experience they will have had with one of our partner services, a partner we neither command nor control.	Closer partnership with suppliers and contractors is a key component to building quality into the process and a good place to start improving things for quick results.

OPPORTUNITY	ISSUE	LEAN APPROACH
Value for money	Customers always want more and are always looking for a better deal: either more functionality for the same price or a simpler service much cheaper. Losing track of value for money is the best way to succumb suddenly to a competitor attack – whether a competing firm or an alternative way to do it.	Reducing costs line by line is the surest way to screw up quality and delivery as well. A better approach to value is to reduce total cost and then reinvest some of these gains into customer value, either in offering more at the same price or in lowering prices.

Again, as we discovered both with improving the quality and throughput of the factory and in halving delivery lead-times at our sales points, the lean trick lies in looking into *singular* problems. Every customer complaint matters because every customer is our first customer – and because their complaints will steer us in improving our understanding of the engineering of our service or product.

From an information point of view, complaints are the information we need to feed into the engineering model of our service in order to improve it.

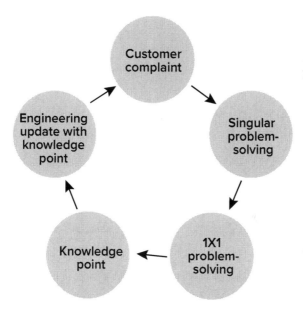

We've found that employee concerns are just as valuable as customer complaints. It's astonishing to think that in any corporate disaster or scandal that you read in the press, someone knew about the problem and either was told to shut up or didn't feel they could speak up. We find this terrifying – what do our employees know today that we badly need to hear about, and what are they not saying because they feel they can't?

One should never underestimate the strength of the knee-jerk "blame someone to cover one's ass" organizational reaction. Recently we were victims of the oldest fraud in the internet playbook. Some wiseguy manipulated one of our accountants, masquerading as Google and finally asking for a change in the bank identification number for next payments. One does not kid around with Google in our business, as it is one of the top marketing channels, so the person did it – it was a fraud. We had to intervene quite strongly to stop management from blaming and punishing the person. If they did that, no one would own up anymore, and we would miss all chance to have a discussion on how to better spot these scams and shout out at the first doubt. And, by the way, because the problem was reported very quickly, we had a chance to block the thief bank account and after months get the money back.

With the fraud case, we had been alerted to a problem and then quickly took action. How can those we're supporting take action just as quickly on their own?

CHAPTER 7:
SEE TOGETHER, THINK TOGETHER, ACT TOGETHER

As we forced ourselves and management to encourage open dialogue – which did not come easily or naturally – we needed tangible ways for staff to follow through with next steps. It wasn't enough that we should know about our singular problems. That would do nothing but give us a very big list of problems. We needed the means for those giving voice to the problems to then promptly deal with them.

THE MAGIC OF VISUALIZATION

To help the branch manager face the delivery problem, we asked our lean manager, Juliette, to practice the lessons we were learning in the production facility. Can of white paint and brush in hand, they visualized what should or should not be occurring:

• *Spaces for the next day's preparation* were painted, into which were placed the cars that were planned to be delivered tomorrow. These slots signaled that cars would move into a finishing touch and be spick and span for customers.

• *Spaces for "delinquents"* were established for cars for which a last-minute problem was discovered that could delay the delivery.

• *All spaces in the parking lot were painted with an address,* allowing us to identify, separate, and track cars that have been held on the lot the longest.

Visualizing car spaces in the production facility

It sounded simple when the sensei outlined the plan, but in real life these things are not easy, as they need to be done while we serve customers and run the business as usual. Yet, once achieved, the results were spectacular. At a glance, at any time, all could see whether the branch was in a good or bad state. Whenever a car that was planned to go into a prep spot was missing, the branch saw it right away when the truck finished unloading what it'd brought. Whenever the truck brought a car not immediately requested, the branch staff had to park it somewhere and wonder what to do about it.

Visualizing the problem turned it into a "normal" problem to be faced and progressively highlighted better daily coordination with central logistics as a new knowledge point. The results: on-time delivery to customers increased from 50% to over 85%. It was stunning.

Working car by car, the branch and central logistics solved a problem we thought could not be solved. All we had done was help the branch manager face the problem by 1) showing it was important by visiting frequently and 2) opening a path to resolution by visualizing the problem.

As we saw in the Toyota plant and then learned for ourselves through painful trial and error (or stumble and pick yourself up again, more likely), visualization is a skill in itself. It requires clarifying the performance that needs improving, identifying the key steps that need to happen for this performance to improve, and then visually creating a "strike zone," a target that visualizes whether you're in or out.

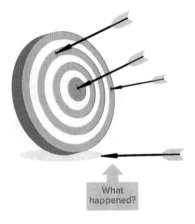

People can treat each missed occurrence as a singular problem to be explored, in search of the hidden knowledge point.

Parking lot before and after visualizing the problems
that disrupted the flow of cars

How does that impact scale-up? Throughout one year, we progressively involved each branch manager in looking at his or her incoming cars. Branch managers were supported by our lean managers Juliette and Cyril, who taught them how to visualize the flow of cars through the premises. Our on-time delivery improved *overall* from a dismal 50% to close to 80% as we visualized problems and discovered new knowledge points.

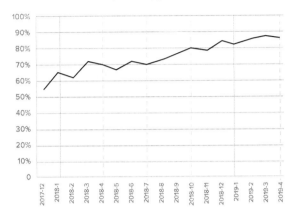

On-time delivery after application of visualization

We discovered new knowledge points, such as controlling truck timetables. This also transformed the day-to-day of agency work in making delivery simple and improving customer interactions. Our customer satisfaction index increased by 40% in that timespan. The most unexpected effect of this work was far from the sales point or logistics ... on the customer-service open space at headquarters. The number of customer complaint calls fell steadily. Also, surprisingly, our internal staff satisfaction measure improved as logistics improved.

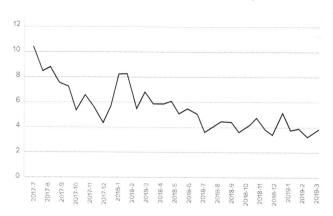

Number of calls to customer service center per order

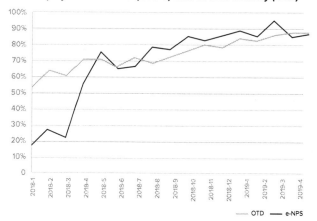

Employee satisfaction (e-NPS) and on-time delivery (OTD)

When we visualized truck timetables, however, we discovered that some trucks were still following old routes that we had never updated. Visualization is the key to discovery and is endlessly surprising. We're always caught flat-footed by what we find that is going wrong – typically something we thought had been resolved a long time ago, but in fact had not.

Visualizing truck timetables to reveal problems

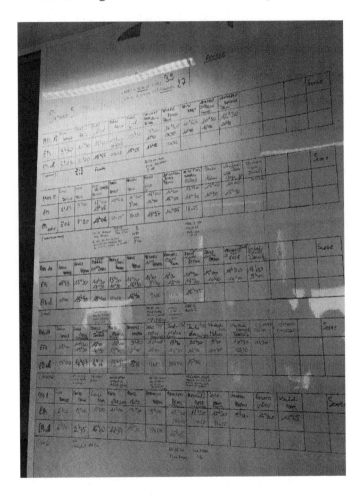

On-time delivery did not get solved in the branches alone. It was a systemic issue involving branches, central logistics, partner trucking companies, and the refurbishment factory. Our central logistics, an airy open plan on the seventh floor of our headquarters with a spectacular view, was mainly staffed with automotive logistics veterans. They earnestly believed that, in their terms, transport was not an exact science and trucks (or truckers for that matter) could not be controlled precisely, as traffic was fundamentally unpredictable. So why bother taking on that problem?

Fortunately, one of our frontline operators, Asmaa, started talking to Zakaria, the newly promoted logistics team leader at the plant. The problem they found was reducing the truck waiting time at the factory, an obvious waste. They estimated the time needed for a truck to load or unload cars on the premises and came up with a target of one hour to turn around a truck (the car-carrying monsters you sometimes pass on the road). They wondered whether they could set precise appointment times for the truck – an idea that was scoffed at by our veteran logisticians.

We have various transport arrangements, and the deal with one trucking company is that they manage trucks and drivers, but we do the scheduling. For these trucks, Asmaa drew out truck routes and began phoning the drivers to see how they were going, progressively getting an idea of regular times at fixed points. She got better at predicting when the truck would reach one of our branches, to unload, reload, and then move on. Meanwhile, Zakaria set out in earnest with visualizing the truck preparation zone and anything he could think of with his teams and the factory to make it easier to find the cars and have them ready for the truck driver to load when he arrived.

Having faced the problem, they both had intense communications with colleagues in the company, both at headquarters and on the site, and negotiations with the drivers, trying to convince them that keeping to appointments would help them load faster, which would mean they could slot one extra transport in their route and, thus, make more money. They also scratched their heads to support the drivers as they could, offering help with mechanical problems (the mechanics in the plant could do that easy enough) and simple gestures of welcome coffee, free water, and so on. Drivers, unused to being considered in that way, began to pay more attention.

All this work was done by better using existing tools. After looking into various problems and facing them – deciding it could be fixed – Asmaa and Zakaria uncovered many critical new knowledge points:

• Better information from the branches about exactly which cars they needed
• Detailed truck routes per truck
• Frequent communication with the drivers
• Setting appointments for the trucks both at the factory and at the branches
• Preparing all cars to be loaded
• Troubleshooting when the traffic did turn out to be unpredictable
• Trustful relationship with partners

By uncovering and mastering these knowledge points, they discovered what Marc had told us about: distinguish predictable from unpredictable, then make the unpredictable – even trucking and traffic – more predictable. As they progressed, logistics old timers left the department through natural attrition, and they hired people that didn't share the same preconceptions and were interested in learning more about the experiment.

We had not deployed a new software. Nor had we restructured logistics. We had not consolidated transport. We had simply taught branch managers to face their delivery problem, visualize it concretely, and work one problem at a time. This was stunning. And we had supported them with attention during gemba walks, offered them the help of our central lean team to make the concrete changes in visualizing the process, and gave them a tool to develop their own staff's problem-solving skills, which made them more comfortable with facing problems on a daily basis.

CLEAN THE WINDOW TO SUSTAIN IMPROVEMENT

We'd achieved a great victory, to be sure, which then revealed ... new problems. Our newfound logistics performance now depended on the discipline of both the factory (easy) and the branches (hard) to keep up the visualization of the car emplacements as well as the visual systems invented by Asmaa at headquarters to follow the trucks, a new headache we'd not seen coming.

Lean veterans have endless mystifying stories about their Japanese sensei insisting on "5S" efforts before anything else. How could cleaning up the factory improve performance? 5S is a lean technique that consists of five Japanese words: seiri, seiton, seiso, seiketsu, and shitsuke, meaning literally eliminate, neatness, cleaning, standardization, and discipline. For convenience's sake, they've become:

• *Sort:* Go through items and decide what is useful, what is not, and what to do about it to reduce clutter. This requires a keep/bin decision.

• *Set in order:* Find a set place for each item and keep them there, so that objects are easily at hand when needed. Systematizing order means visualizing places and creating a system to manage space. It requires practical thinking to make your arrangement support the flow of work by having the most used items close at hand.

• *Shine:* Keep all items clean and tidy, which, in fact, calls for fixing problems as issues are discovered. This is also the opportunity to question again sort (should we keep it or get rid of it) and the appropriateness of the set-in-order arrangement.

• *Standardize:* Find the right rhythm and procedures to keep the first 3 Ss shipshape at all times. Standardizing means getting team agreements about simple rules on how to use items, how to place them back in order, and how to clear and clean the workspace.

• *Sustain:* There is no end to the 4S process, but force of habit and daily mishaps unavoidably make the disciplines come and go. The self-discipline of the fifth S can be supported by leadership's interest in 5S and approval of a good state of the workplace.

In a command-and-control mindset, 5S is reduced to spick and span – keep things neat and tidy looking because certainly that's better – isn't it? In a challenge-and-support perspective, we're looking to something very different. We need team ownership of its workplace to maintain the discipline of problem visualization.

The 5Ss are critical knowledge points to run a physical workplace and motivate one's team to care. Just as your morning routine is what enables you to face the day, 5S routines prep teams to face their day. Without 5S proficiency, problem visualization simply fades away, and results disappear as a result. Problem visualization is demanding because it requires facing the problem every day all the time. Without a deep understanding of how to control the physicality of the workspace, "strike zones" are easily subverted or abandoned as we see every day when we visit sites. 5S discipline builds up the team leader's muscle to work with their teams in keeping their workspace in the right conditions to continue to face the problem and progress. Without 5S, no problem visualization. Without problem visualization, results start backsliding.

At first, we struggled to make our people see how relevant 5S was to a digital company. But one of our IT teams took this on board and started looking at its databases: Which databases do we use in what order? Can we simplify them? Is this code block still useful? Are there any important planned tasks we're deleting by mistake? As the team started deleting code, it was looking actively to see what would not have an impact and what would create unexpected bugs in other applications. After a few false starts, they created a ritual (S4 – standardize) to clean up one code block at a time and work with colleagues on the coding implications of what works where and what should be placed where. In doing so, they were at the same time making the code easier to work with, improving the team's skills in designing software, and making error-prone parts of the code base more visible.

5S is also important for leadership to show support. In practicing 5S, the team will find new problems every day. Some they can solve; some they need help with. To help teams be more at ease with the challenge of facing problems, we can support them in 1) becoming more autonomous in their problem-solving and 2) eliminating roadblocks that are outside of their sphere of influence (such as headquarters).

TEACHING AUTONOMY IN PROBLEM-SOLVING

A growth culture requires high-road thinking. A fixed culture fosters low-road reactions. People solve problems at work all the time, but the question is which problems they choose to solve.

• Do they focus on sustaining the continuity of customer satisfaction? Or do they obsess with their position in the food chain and defend their processes to deflect any blame?

• Do they look for smart ways to solve concrete problems with their teams? Or do they jump to red-herring unfeasible solutions and try to make the problem go away?

When you look in from the outside, the difference is obviously visible. But for the person handling the problem, both feel the same. Both feel right, natural, justified. There is no emotional marker to distinguish the high road from the low road. If we want to encourage a growth culture based on high-road problem-solving, we have to educate all our staff to recognize the difference between the former and the latter.

To move from the low road of problem workaround to the high road of autonomous problem-solving, we can continuously work at the mastery of these knowledge points. To do so, the sensei suggested we draw simple boards in each team to visualize the problem-solving process:

Date	Describe the Problem	Look for the Root Cause	Test/Study a Counter-measure	Estimate the Impact

The idea was not to list every problem encountered. Our strategy was not to solve every problem in pursuit of a perfectly operating process as one would pull grains of sand out of a machine. Our strategy was to develop every person's problem-solving ability to become more precise in the way we handled unexpected situations.

For instance, imagine a car delivered too late at the sales point, causing the customer appointment to be rescheduled. Romain, the commercial VP (now the head of French operations), assumed that his staff simply didn't use the Excel sheet set up to properly calculate the correct delivery date, retro-planning it from the appointment date. Looking into how teams formulated the problem on the boards and what countermeasures they came up with, he discovered that the tool had to be updated daily by logistics, who sometimes forgot to do it (not a core task for them) – creating false information in the system. This led to deeper collaboration with logistics and emphasizing the importance of date accuracy, as well as looking at how to better build it in the system itself. Problems such as this one can't all be "pulled out" of the system as pins off a cushion – you solve one, another appears. The difference is in developing the problem-solving and teamwork abilities so that people react faster and find smarter solutions when they do encounter such issues.

Each team leader would lead the examination of a solved problem and encourage a team member to present how they'd done it and support a team discussion over it. Over time, we have found five key points to focus upon when teaching problem-solving:

1. *Orientation to customer:* Customers change from one to the next, but your boss is always your boss, and your colleagues remain your colleagues. The pull to express problems in terms of responding to hierarchy's demands or sorting team issues is continuous and endless – and perfectly normal. "How is the customer impacted" is the orientation question that always needs to be asked to turn people towards the flow of value rather than the flow of instructions. As leaders, we find that asking that question over and over again is one of the most effective things we can do to build a growth culture and remind our staff of what makes the company grow and succeed: customers' opinions of us – and what they say to their friends.

2. *Formulating problems:* On many visualization boards, we see problem statements that only indicate "this went wrong" – which is not a problem statement. We need to teach our teams to formulate problems as "this went wrong *because* of that." A gap in performance is explained by a gap in process. The difference might seem trivial, but the aim of formulating problems is *facing* them. A problem is not an "opportunity," as the saying goes. It is a situation that must be resolved, which means explaining what we think is the proximal cause in the problem statement – the most obvious cause to start with before digging further.

3. Seeking root cause: Why did the ship sink? Because it got breached under the waterline and water entered the hull, which became denser than water and could no longer float. This is the proximal cause. But why was the hull pierced? Because it hit a rock that tore a hole open in the hull. Why did it hit the rock? Because the skipper misread the chart and was not where he thought he was. Why did the skipper misread the chart? Because he'd been distracted with an engine problem and lost track of where the boat was on the water. In seeking root causes, we are looking for the "real" reason the problem occurred – which is, of course, subjective. What we are really looking for is a knowledge point we could have handled better. Where did we go wrong? What could we have done differently? How will we handle a similar situation next time? There is no right or wrong answer to root causes – the point is pushing the teams to think deeper beyond symptoms and discover syndromes:

things they think are natural and good and they do all the time but that are in fact causing problems.

4. Try something to correct the situation: How do we pacify the customer? How do we mitigate the impact of the problem? It happened; how do we get back on track? Thinking of countermeasures is about encouraging inventiveness and initiative in the team. The best countermeasures solve the problem fundamentally, but that is a nice thing to have. What we're really looking for here is care for the customer and ingenuity in addressing the problem – or simple common sense. Countermeasures are essential to give the team confidence that they can cope with problems and problems are not something to hide from – or to hide from others. By facing problems together, we think of smart ways of mitigating effects and addressing root causes.

5. Study countermeasures: As a customer, how often has a company offered you a voucher to compensate for a wrong they've done and, in doing so, just pissed you off even further? Some countermeasures have a positive impact on customers. Others simply make sure customers go away, will never come back, and tell all their friends. Studying our countermeasures is *how we learn*.

Start from the customer

⬊ Formulate problems as gaps of
performance explained as gaps of process

⬊ Seek the root cause,
i.e., the missing knowledge point

⬊ Try something to correct
the situation

⬊ Study the effects of
contermeasures

When the sensei challenged us on each step of the problem-solving process, we felt he was demanding perfect logic, as if there were a rational ideal to solving problems. It took us a while to realize that he was challenging *motivation:* Were people serious and keen to solve their customer's problem and think more deeply about how they worked? Or were they going through the motions to kick the ball down the path and divert blame to some other part of the organization?

We are taught to think of problem-solving as a logical, brainy exercise. And yes, analytical reasoning is important, obviously. But autonomy in problem-solving is also largely emotional. People need to feel the pain, the dissatisfaction, and feel the need to do something about it. They must resist the temptation to jump to solutions or deflect the problem. They must enjoy the negotiation process of finding a path with others. In other words, they must *face* the problem before looking for a solution.

PROBLEM-BASED LEARNING

As we progressively established problem-solving boards across the company and taught team leaders to use them regularly, we also learned a lot more about what made the technique so effective. By focusing on knowledge points, we now knew that performance would improve only if the teams discovered more precise knowledge points and learned to master them – learning had to be specific and domain-dependent.

Facing a problem and trying to formulate new and better solutions (not rehashed red herrings) both activates existing knowledge and opens the way for elaboration of what is known. People's experience and ideas are triggered by the problem and come to mind, and so they also try to look beyond what they already know and explore:

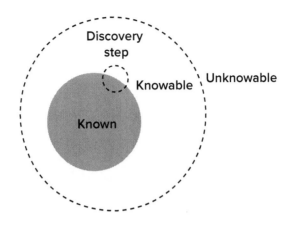

Discovery requires motivation because it's a real effort, particularly in busy lives and roles where we are easily overwhelmed by to-do lists and to-be-done jobs. Setting up problem-solving as a legitimate, necessary, and mandatory activity and scheduling it accordingly are essential to creating the social interest in which people will feel motivated to make the effort: they will be expected to report on their analyses, whether they feel it's worth their while or not.

However, the trick to problem-based learning is self-directed learning – the magic occurs when people are not there, not part of the group discussion, but exploring or experimenting on their own. Learning really occurs when someone reads a book, looks more into the details of an issue, and/or tries something new. This is always a personal and solitary activity – and only works if the person is self-directed, which means that they're doing it because it's interesting to them, not because they have to.

Clearly, self-directed learning can be supported by better methods or better coaching – both methods and coach act as scaffolding for the learning – but ultimately only the person can learn, through their own efforts. There is no way around it. Knowledge points emerge from people's personal efforts to look for them – and later share them. And because we're touching this emotional core, every challenge of the left-brain reasoning must be balanced by huge amounts of approbation for the effort or reasoning itself to soothe the right-brain feeling of threat or attack. Sadly, we often fall short. Employee engagement experts claim that positive attention is 30 times more powerful than negative attention.[16] Since criticism is unavoidable in discussing problem-solving, we need to remind ourselves constantly to support the team leader and the team in giving positive attention to the problem-solving effort itself.

[16] M. Buckingham & A. Goodall (2019). *Nine Lies about Work,* Harvard Business Review Press, Brighton, MA.

FACING PROBLEMS TOGETHER IS THE STEPPING STONE TO A GROWTH CULTURE

Three months after starting regular gemba walks, we were stunned to realize that we had not precisely understood a large part of the extraordinary job our associates were doing to improve the overall OTD. During our regular visits, they showed us detailed problems that seemed so singular we didn't quite get it. We encouraged and supported them as best as we could. We approved of all their efforts. But, at the end of the day, *they taught us.* They found problems, they faced them, they solved issues bit by bit, and they discovered the critical knowledge points that delivered the performance increase.

Better OTD, we realized, led us to reduce lead-times to customers, so that we could offer a true competitive advantage, changing our promise from a car in 15 days to a car in less than a week, aiming for 48 hours. This, of course, would generate new difficulties, but now that we had faced the problem together, we knew it could be cracked – and as with the factory throughput, radically change the shape of our scale-up. It was a business breakthrough; we now can deliver cars in 24 hours.

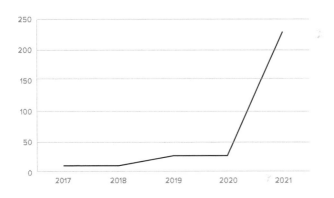

Evolution of the number of 24-hour deliveries

Looking back on the knowledge points the team had to crack, Alejandro, our head of supply chain who led this breakthrough effort, distinguishes three main topics: pull flow of cars, truck control, and accelerating the information flow:

CHALLENGE	KNOWLEDGE POINTS
Pull flow of cars	• **Displaying on the site cars with reliable lead-times – if uncertain, the car is not offered to customers** • **Shipping to our sites only the cars for next day delivery to customers** • **Solving car-registry issues that stopped physical delivery of the car** • **Working closely with operators preparing cars to support them in guaranteeing quality and timeliness of delivery**

CHALLENGE	KNOWLEDGE POINTS
Truck control	• Setting clear timetable objectives for trucks • Reducing variability in arrival and waiting for trucks on sites • Eliminating pain points for truck drivers to make their work easier on our routes and sites
Acceleration of information flows	• Reducing dependency on postal systems (delays) • Accelerating financing by focusing on simplifying paperwork and waiting

It sounds obvious in hindsight, but each of these knowledge points had to be discovered the hard way by the team (problems seldom present themselves so neatly packaged and have to be unraveled case by case) who then had to learn the tricks of the trade to master these issues. This was daily, rigorous, and persistent work from each team member and superb collaboration!

Spending time visiting our own workplaces made us realize that our employees experience the same things daily: they do their job as best they can and try to correct wrongs as they see them, negotiating with their environment and keeping track of whether they were winning or losing ground. We're learning to respect that people see things as they see things and do their best to change them according to their lights. Very often they see things we don't see and know things we don't know.

The sensei showed us that in focusing on problems, people could orient in two different ways. They could look towards customers and seek to redress the wrongs that made it hard for them to maintain the continuity of customer satisfaction, the roadblocks that made answering specific customer requests so hard. In essence, this means looking along the flow of value towards customers and aiming to improve every step so that each customer can be treated with the same care and effort as our first customer. Or, alternatively, they could treat customers as a given (one follows another) and orient towards their place in the company's food chain and how to protect their position, negotiate a better deal for themselves, and use their influence or power to defend the status quo.

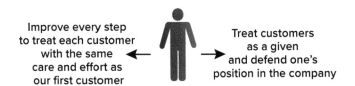

The sensei also showed us we could influence this simply by "go and see" and "challenge." As he explained, cognitive psychology tells us that people don't pay attention to what they consider important; they consider important what they pay attention to. By influencing orientation, you can influence what people value. In a typical case, we discovered during gemba walks that some sales points routinely pressured customers to come and pick up their car early to respond to the finance department's constant questions about cash flow. The sales outlets were never directly incentivized on cash flow. But it became important for no other reason than finance regularly drew attention to it – more important than putting customers first. This got corrected simply by showing up at the gemba and telling staff that, yes, cash was important for the business and a normal priority of the CFO, but that our attention should remained focused on the *complete satisfaction* of every customer.

By challenging people to face problems with us, we can influence what problems they take on. By supporting them as they solve the problems, through both approbation of their efforts and removing internal roadblocks, we can facilitate the negotiation process. By implementing better visual management and problem visualization, we can sustain the ongoing monitoring of solutions and, thus, lead teams to discover and own new knowledge points, which, collectively, create higher performance.

The secret to a successful scale-up is to obtain everyone's voluntary participation in improving quality, reducing lead-times, and reducing total costs. To do so, as leaders, we need to develop a growth culture as the antidote of the fixed culture that grips every company as they specialize and bureaucratize. A culture that aims to bring value to customers through engagement and initiative in simplifying work, as opposed to the traditional obsession with power to maintain one's advantage over customers, colleagues, and suppliers – as is still mainly taught in business schools. Going to the gemba to *find* problems (and help people *visualize* their processes to do so) is the first step of creating a growth culture. Facing problems with the teams is the pivotal moment that makes it all possible. As we are leaders, this meant abandoning the command-and-control habits we'd grown up with (solving problems ourselves, giving instructions, and making sure they were followed through) and, instead, learning to challenge and support people's own insights and initiatives on singular problems, helping them learn, knowledge point by knowledge point, how to perform spectacularly better.

CHAPTER 8:
PRACTICE TEAMWORK

P rogress on customer lead-time had been astounding: we'd halved the time between order to delivery (at that time, we were still far from 24-hour delivery). Then came Christmas. Unbeknownst to us, logistics and sales tacitly decided to backslide on the promise to maintain their on-time delivery score through the season, when logistics get a little screwy. At the same time, Amazon was upping the ante and promising to deliver even faster. What was going on?

As we took a cold, hard look at the company, we found many other examples of regress on our initial gains. After a sustained stretch of encouraging progress, we found ourselves facing a challenge that the sensei had warned us about: backsliding. After making quick initial headway from teams finding and facing problems, then solving them piecemeal, we were facing numerous setbacks. The frontline team hit a performance high spot, but then reversed to the mean, got discouraged, and we had to boost them up again. We worried: were all these efforts for nothing if performance improvements could not be maintained?

On car delivery, the backslide had started even before the Christmas debacle. We had achieved huge progress with delivering cars to the outlets the day before customers would come and take delivery. This was a transforming capability in that it could radically change our marketing offer and place us miles ahead of the competition. But then, Romain, the commercial VP, and Alejandro, head of supply chain, moved on to other pressing issues, assuming the new "process" was firmly in place; they took their eyes off the ball. As a matter of fact, many detailed issues remained beyond "deploying the pull flow of cars." Outlets struggled with receiving the car on day minus one, and their managers started quietly negotiating with logistics on day minus two, or day minus three. As staff incrementally dealt with delays, on-time delivery started backsliding without anyone exploring and really knowing why.

During a gemba walk in a sales outlet, Romain realized that the cars were no longer being delivered just-in-time. In the spring of 2019, average lead-time to delivery was 18 days and on-time delivery at 79%, which were, historically, great results. By the fall, lead-time was at 20 days and OTD at 75% – clear backsliding. Back at headquarters, Romain and Alejandro went back to logistics to reinforce the need to deliver on day minus one, and to discover all the specific complaints from various outlet managers, who felt they did not have the flexibility to receive cars on the previous day, particularly with heavy delivery days such as Saturdays. They also discovered that many cars arrived with bodywork or electronics issues, and the outlet needed time to fix that. When everyone had recovered from the Christmas season, Romain and Alejandro brought their teams together to find and face the problems, which resulted in lead-time improvement of a day a month (now on average at 15 days), the best the company has ever achieved, with an OTD of 80%.

A key point of day-minus-one delivery was that the outlet should not have to fix any last-minute quality problems. First, we were not sure the outlet would solve them well. Second, our delivery flow should deliver impeccable quality at each state. With this in mind, Alejandro and Romain worked with both logistics and outlet staffs on issues one by one, and performance recovered, but this kind of backslide was happening all over the place in areas where we had made quite surprising and visible progress.

"Why?" asked the sensei. "Find out why. Why are you backsliding?" Back to problem-finding. The problems we encountered were so bizarre – singular beyond singular – that we had trouble making heads or tails of them. The factory backslid because they ran short of mechanics: No body specialists. No fine-tuning experts. On the gemba, it seemed like there was not one competent mechanic in the entire region. We went to go and see in HR, and they confirmed that, yes, indeed, some positions hadn't been staffed for months because they couldn't find anyone – no one responded to the ads. It didn't make sense – we were a high-profile employer offering a good deal in a region with high unemployment.

Another strange problem was a shortage of cars to sell. The work on the pull flow had spectacularly improved delivery. For a while, we then found ourselves in the ridiculous position of earning cash because we delivered but were, in fact, selling less because our car pipeline – the cars offered on the site – was drying up. And many people were blaming lean. When we asked in an internal survey if lean had helped the company progress, the executive team answered a clear "Yes," the commercial branches a qualified "Yes" (they experienced many of the benefits from the work on processes), but the rest of headquarters employees were strikingly noncommittal.

When we read through specific comments, the two main themes were 1) we don't understand what you're trying to do, and 2) lean is fine to get initial gains, but why ask us to continue to dig into subjects when the results have been obtained? As well as the normal gripes about not having enough time to do the normal job, we were told that being asked to participate in improvement projects was asking too much – a clear symptom of the fixed-culture legacy we were fighting.

When we finally got to the bottom of the hiring problem at the plant, we learned that HR had centralized the plant's HR function at headquarters and ran it from there. The pipeline issue turned out to come from weird pressure from finance on cash (as a result of a lean misconception, ironically), and rather than feed the pipeline, our buyers had become overly cautious on the margin per car. In both cases, the functional decisions made perfect sense. Obviously, you can't ask someone to spend half their time at the capital and the other half at a site that was three hours away by train. Obviously, margin per car is a key driver of our business – if we get that wrong, we become unprofitable.

But none of these decisions helped the frontline teams that were trying to sustain a continuity of customer satisfaction.

Time to face the problem. When we started to really listen, we learned that frontline teams were working hard on improvements but had to constantly deal with pushback from headquarters or other functions. As leaders, we were succeeding at challenging our teams, but failing at supporting them. We had found another elephant in the room that no one wanted to look at.

The sensei's theory was that although some of our associates were fixing things at the coalface, our middle-management policies were not changing as fast, so the business acted as a rubber band that pulled everything back constantly. A clear case was the work by Asmaa and Zakaria to sort out the flow of cars to the branches. We discovered that while they were trying to improve that, which was far from easy, they were also under pressure to reduce the vehicle transport cost. Interestingly, this was not a clear, direct instruction. Everyone felt it had to be done, somehow, but the directive or policy could not be pinpointed. Alejandro maintained he had never given such instruction. Now, clearly, transport cost is a critical line in our budget.

But, strangely, by managing transport more carefully, we were convinced we'd be reducing transport cost altogether by improving the overall productivity of transport – as a result of delivering better to the sites. Yes, transport cost had to be monitored. Absolutely. But two other things were clear: 1) we did not want to add cost-control pressure to the work the people on the ground were doing to improve on-time delivery, and 2) we could not identify the source of the instruction that said, "optimize the cost per vehicle." We were well and truly puzzled.

TEAMWORK IS A VERB, NOT A NOUN

Backsliding is a failure of *teamwork*, the sensei argued. When a team fixes a problem locally, it needs to be supported by both the hierarchy and the other functional departments. When you look into an improvement on the gemba, be sure to ask: *what else* needs to change for this new way of doing things to stick? The question then is: how to convince other people to change their minds?

As Taiichi Ohno reminds us, people need to understand and agree in order to change their own way of thinking and doing. Indeed, the first chapter of his book *Workplace Management* is titled "The Wise Mend Their Ways." He writes that "engineers, in particular, tend to hold on tightly to things they have said or to their ideas. Engineers are often said to be inflexible or stubborn, but I think it is important for them to quickly correct themselves, just as the wise men mend their ways." In the second chapter, "If You Are Wrong, Admit It," the sensei reveals the trick to achieving admission lies in learning to frame problems correctly in order to support teamwork – solving problems across functional boundaries.[17]

We used to think of teamwork as a *property* of teams – something that emerges when the team comes together and gels ... somehow. The sensei saw teamwork as something one *did* in order to make the team come together – a verb, not a noun. Just as respect for one person's opinions and development is an action that one can practice through better listening (Tell me more?) and through caring about the person's progress (Why aren't they at the next level? What *is* the next level *they* aim for?), teamwork in lean is *active*. It doesn't happen on its own.

[17] T. Ohno, (1988). *Workplace Management,* Productivity Press, Cambridge, MA.

In that sense, framing a problem is both intellectual, inasmuch as it clarifies the problem to solve and the type of solution sought, and emotional: it creates the space for discussion – or lack of it. Framing sets the situation both in terms of problem to solve and space to think.

We remembered how, in 2015, just as we were scratching our heads to find a way out of our scale-up issues, we heard about Google using its formidable data analysis capability to answer the question, "What makes a Google team effective?" Over two years, a group of Google researchers plunged into more than 200 employee interviews, testing more than 250 attributes on more than 180 Google teams. They were expecting confirmation of Google's cultural assumption that smart creatives drive performance and that gifted engineers tend to have difficult personalities, and there was some perfect mix of individual traits and skills to combine in making a dream team.[18]

After much groping in the dark and finding nothing, they hit upon a different frame: *who* is on the team

[18] J. Rozovsky (Nov. 17, 2015). "The Five Keys to a Successful Google Team," re: Work. https://rework.withgoogle.com/blog/five-keys-to-a-successful-google-team/

matters less than how team members interact, structure their work, and view their contribution. Trust, it turns out, is the magic ingredient that makes team turn to teamwork:

- **Trust in relationships:** The two critical factors of trust in the team relationship turned out to be 1) psychological safety (can we take risks on this team without feeling insecure or embarrassed?) and 2) dependability (can we count on others to do high-quality work on time?).

- **Trust of intent:** The team also needed clarity on three points: 1) structure and clarity (are goals and execution plans on our team clear?), 2) meaning of work (are we working on something that is personally important for each of us?), and 3) impact of work (do we fundamentally believe that the work we're doing matters?).

- **Trust in competence:** Dependability involves counting on everyone to produce quality work. Beyond trusting commitments, and the fact that people are serious about delivering when they said so, teams must also trust in the quality of the work and the astuteness of the solutions proposed – be confident the work won't have to be done again.

TRUST IN RELATIONSHIPS

We trust the people we like (too much so, and this is how we get conned). At work, the question is how to trust people beyond *like* – trust people we work with given that we'd probably not spontaneously want to have a beer with them. Beyond liking people, which defies rational explanation, we're also constantly monitoring their intent towards us and their ability to carry out this intent – which is why some gemba walk conversations between the founders, the VP, the middle manager, and the team members get awkward – that's a lot of hierarchy to handle. Many don't feel free to speak up.

If teamwork is an active verb, what can we do on the gemba to increase relationship trust? Lean theory argues for showing respect: making our best efforts to understand the person's point of view. This generally involves not trying to control the conversation:

1. Just listen: Don't immediately argue back or seek too hasty clarification – listen. This is not easy, because most people will need to be challenged before they speak up. If not, they just stay mum. But when they do say something, they need space, encouragement, and visible approbation. This often means asking the middle manager to let them speak as they will often jump in to try to control the conversation.

2. Let emotion pass: When people care about a topic and when they're unsure of the social space to address it, they will express themselves emotionally, either too timidly or too brashly. It's important to know that a valued topic activates the frontal cortex, which often triggers emotions and requires a conscious effort to stay cool. The degree of emotion doesn't necessarily reflect conflict, other than the very real difficulty of saying things out loud.

3. Don't use what they say against them: As a senior manager, it is tempting to jump on something someone has said and try to correct the situation, only to then make matters worse. People have to trust that what they say stays in the safe place and is not used against them – even meaning well. Check if they want you do something about it. If not, think over the situation and review your own misconceptions, but don't be too quick to react unless they've specifically asked for help. They might not see your intervention as beneficial.

4. Say thank you (and mean it): Thank them for the conversation. This is something we never do enough.

Our rule of thumb is at least a "thank you" a day. "Thank you" goes a long way. Approbation remains the strongest motivator we know.

5. *Watch out for bad apples:* Some folk are toxic, and that's that. It's not that frequent, but some people are energy (and trust) sinks. They'll turn every positive into a negative. They can do a lot of damage in a team if the team leader doesn't know how to handle them – and immense damage if they get a management job.

6. *Ask for something specific you can fix:* Is there one thing they've been trying to get done that the company responds sluggishly to and that is easy for you to solve?

The lean approach to creating a safe relationship space is solving specific problems together. In the early days, when Toyota was trying to set up a network of suppliers in Europe to support their first transplant factory in the UK, their purchasing team would visit many supplier operations. At the end of the visit, in which they typically did not say much and never discussed business, they would thank their hosts for the tour and then catch them off guard with a ridiculous list of things they could improve. Imagine 117 random items that could be fixed in the factory. Most suppliers simply ignored them and went back to running the plant – and never heard from Toyota again.

The list of singular items was not about improving performance right away, but about testing the relationship. As the sensei discussed with us on the first day, Toyota was looking for people who were willing to do kaizen, willing to listen, able/equipped to take on seemingly random items that obviously needed improvement, and willing to work on them. Some of the issues on the list were easy, some not (to test the suppliers' technical abilities), and some deceptively complex, such as suggesting better 5S.

The idea is to treat trust as stemming from three knowledge points: temperament (how people react), will (are they willing to move), and skill (do they know what they are doing). Singular problem-solving gives you opportunity after opportunity to figure this out and adapt, in order to progressively build a safe space for people to speak up and not have to wear the company face. Teamwork is work.

FRAMING MATTERS

Framing is the key tool of teamwork, the sensei told us. Framing of a situation or a problem is what creates shared intent. People are natural problem solvers – they will be spontaneously motivated to solve the problem as they see it, both in terms of "what" and "how." The *way* people define the situation has real effects. Frames are the terms in which we describe anything, like a picture frame through which we look at something. If someone blinks: have they got dust in their eye, or are they winking at someone? Different frames. Frames are set and partial and how our mind works. Frames, in practice, are an angle of views, a perspective, which people convey through opinions, anecdotes, stereotypes, and theories. They determine how we interpret things. In other terms, a frame is a view one applies forcefully and often unconsciously to the messiness of everyday things to make sense of it all.

Toyota sensei are skilled framers. Our sensei is full of stories from the glory days of the *Toyota Production System*, describing how a sensei does something outrageous to brutally reframe how people see the scene. One sensei, by example, walked into an assembly cell where an operator was walking to pick up a component from a large bin on wheels and pushed the bin away from the guy – across the alley. The absurd situation this created immediately woke everyone up to how and where components were located in the operator's work cycle and how much wasteful walking was involved. Another sensei ripped out the cable from an automatic conveyor in a semiautomated line and stayed there with the plant manager, looking at how peopled managed by hand without the conveyor. In the Porsche lean turnaround, the first thing the sensei asked for was to cut all shelving to a 120 cm height so that people could see each other.[19] Our own sensei has picked up the annoying habit of talking to parts as if they were people: "Have you been waiting long? Why are you seated here? Are they treating you well? Did they tell you when they'll come for you?" Thankfully, we learned that framing did not always need to be as provocative.

Framing is a key part of teamwork because, if done well, it allows everyone to understand the problem we're collectively trying to solve and, thus, see how they can contribute at their level. Without a strong frame, people remain prisoners of their functional frames and blinded to what is going on by the imperative to do

[19] J. Womack & D. Jones (1996). *Lean Thinking*, The Free Press.

their job. Framing defines the overall mission beyond specialist objectives:

Practice teamwork :
get people to help each other in solving problems across functional borders

Frame problems so that everyone understands the shared intent and sees how they can participate at their level

Innovation often comes from changing frames. By asking the right question, one gets to a different answer. For instance, we changed the frame of the car sales business from "push the metal" (sell the cars) to "facilitate purchase." And we did so by using the opportunities of digital to take away pain points for buyers.

Our frame was:

- *What:* Facilitate purchase
- *How:* through digital simplification, connectivity, automation, and prediction
- *Why:* to change how people buy and sell their cars and grow the company.

It was a radical reframe at the time and a fortunate one – we got very successful with it. A frame is a simplified map of the situation, with a given direction. Like all maps, it highlights certain features and ignores others. It tells people what to look out for and which way to go.

The power of frames was revealed in one of our gemba walks with the sensei at a sales point. We (at headquarters) felt that some Google ratings at our sales points were average to poor – not great news for a digital company. We then instructed sales point leaders to improve the grade by looking at negative comments, trying to understand the source of customers' dissatisfaction, consoling upset customers if we could, and fixing the deeper problems.

During the gemba walk, we discovered they had instead set up a computer in a visible spot with the outlet's web page open. Staff would twist happy customers' arms to get them to write a positive comment with a five-star ranking in order to get the overall grade to go up. A classic case of trying to move the needle rather than fixing the problem, or, less charitably, trying to game the system by addressing the symptom rather than attempting to understand and solve the deeper issues. Then they told us several other agencies were doing the same – so it was all OK. As we asked "Why?" we were met by obstinate silence. They didn't understand what we were asking of them. We were looking at two different frames:

- *What:* Improve the Google grade
- *How:* by asking happy customers to fill in the form while you've got them at hand and in a good mood
- *Why:* to achieve what we've been asked in a simple, feasible, and immediate manner.

Versus

- *What:* Improve the Google grade
- *How:* by looking at low grades and negative comments, fixing customers dissatisfiers, and letting customer grade as and if they want
- *Why:* to learn how to satisfy customers better and grow the business in a long-term way.

As we had seen before, people framed complex problems by narrowing them to the part they felt they could control. We had seen it in problem-finding and -facing. Now we understood better how that happened.

We are no different, however, the sensei argued. When discussing whether the sales-point manager felt responsible for his Google grade, he had us pull out a sheet of paper and draw a line across it. He asked us to list all the outputs we feel responsible for. (Humor us: try this mental experiment yourself, not what the company asks for, not your objectives, but what you, personally, feel you have to deliver.)

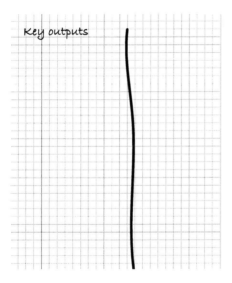

Now, the sensei asked: did you think of any people development goals?

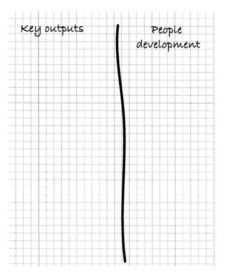

Key outputs	People development

Here's what our sheet looks like:

Key outputs	People development
Change how people buy and sell their cars A better deal and a more pleasant experience	
Build something big! Profitable growth that will keep us independent	
Cash positive	
Improve the environment by facilitating purchase of greener cars	
A pleasant, hassle-free work environment	

Not one clear, explicit objective about developing people, although we had been discussing nothing else for months on end and getting the results from having changed our approach. We had not really changed our own frames. Frames are hard to change, explained the sensei. Once a pattern is set in your mind, you can change it, but be aware it will also keep popping up. Like quitting smoking, he added wistfully. You can stop smoking but you can't stop feeling like having a cigarette. The impulse wanes over time, but it will pop back at random moments – or in times of stress.

DISCOVERY VERSUS DELIVERY

Now that we thought about it, we saw that frames intervened all the time in the way the business ran. Guillaume, our marketing VP, had coined the "discovery versus delivery" frame, and he was absolutely right. We started the company with a discovery frame (let's try it and find out), and this had evolved to a delivery frame (do the job and all will be fine) – now we were trying to introduce a balance between delivery and discovery. In fact, lean had taught us that discovery happened by studying delivery and separating the predictable from the unpredictable – another powerful frame.

Delivery is a natural frame for anyone working in a large company. Delivery is reliable. It's neat. It's familiar, and no one can ever blame you for spending time and effort on delivering more. Discovery, on the other hand, is muddled, unfamiliar, and uncertain. One of us was taken to task by a junior team leader for spending time on a kaizen effort and challenging existing processes. "Surely," she argued, "people need to be clear about what they're doing, and it's better to follow the process than to challenge everything all the time."

Indeed, she's right – following the process will deliver better than improvising any time. But the catch is that in order to make the process consistently deliver customer satisfaction at lower global cost and with the best experience for associates, we have to explore all the instances of improvisation. In other words, we need to maintain a constant balance between discovery and delivery. It should be easier for senior people, but then they tend to get more certain of what they know, more set in their ways, and shun discovery for different reasons. They're happy to explore as long as it is in topics where they feel comfortable and where they know, again, they'll deliver. The balance between discovery and delivery is never resolved, which is why having the discovery (kaizen first) versus delivery (kaizen when the rest of the job is done) frame is so useful: it keeps the debate alive.

At the individual level, we also realized the difference between a fixed culture and a growth culture could be represented as another set of frames:

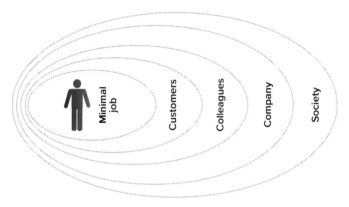

What was each of our employees looking at? What did they feel responsible for? Doing their minimum job? Solving customer problems? Working well with their colleagues across functional barriers? Taking initiative for the best of the company? Thinking of how to benefit society? These were vastly different, overlapping frames, leading to widely diverging conclusions. We also understood that frames are sticky, and that people could look up and broaden their horizon but would, nevertheless, always look back to the narrowest frame, particularly if they felt stressed or overburdened. Backsliding was inevitable. We needed to find countermeasures.

PEOPLE NEED TO SHARE THEIR THINKING TO BUILD TRUST

At any time, anyone of us is caught on the horns of a dilemma (even if we are reluctant to admit it): try harder to help our customers and collaborate with our colleagues to do so, or do the minimum job to satisfy our boss and play politics to secure our position. No organizational setup bypasses this simple quandary, because the defining factor is trust. Trust is the glue that makes people buy into the shared intent and stick to the collective plan. Trust is what makes anyone help the next person, be it customer or colleague, or take care of ourselves first and keep one's head down. In lean, mutual trust between management and employees is the foundation of the famed *Toyota Production System* from which lean is inspired.

When we reflected on our backsliding problem, we saw that orienting and supporting in our regular gemba walks at the workplace had done wonders for the trust that several of our employees had on the seriousness of our intent and our ability to deliver and help them where they needed support. As a result, we had pockets of people doing an incredible job – but that trust had not spread to the company as a whole and particularly not across functional boundaries. The next step was to create greater trust both vertically and horizontally so that people felt more secure on improving things at their level:

- *Vertically:* Demonstrate that middle managers could respond to frontline improvements by changing their own methods of running the department to sustain the new way of working, and, thus, show greater respect for their teams' problem-solving efforts, beyond encouragement.
- *Horizontally:* Improve cooperation across functional barriers so that people could see that all functions worked to improve the flow of value to customers rather than compete fruitlessly in blame and turf contests.

Our first instinct was that to trust each other more, people needed to spend more time together. The sensei had doubts. He felt that forcing people who didn't trust each other to rub shoulders more often would lead them to be more polite to each other but not necessarily more trustful.

The lean way, he argued, is to have managers share their *thinking* – how they frame the problem. Teamwork, he said, is the act of solving problems together across functional boundaries. Framing is the entry point to trust as it fleshes out shared intent in a way everyone can understand – and choose to participate. No one will commit to something they don't first understand. More persuasive frames were not the end of the matter, but the beginning, the working tool with which trust could be pursued, both in terms of framing intent and creating safe spaces to think and discuss. His suggestion was to have our senior managers solve specific problems and share their thinking explicitly, regularly, and frequently. But how could we do that?

THE SECRET TO TOYOTA'S SUCCESS

Once more, this seemed too far-fetched to work. We were mulling it over when we had the opportunity to meet Isao Yoshino, a veteran manager from Toyota who had built from scratch the program to engage American workers in Toyota's kaizen way of working at the NUMMI[20] plant in California. The plant was a joint venture between Toyota and General Motors that

---

[20] New United Motor Manufacturing Inc.

became famous in the 1980s because Toyota agreed to take over the management of GM's worst plant and conceded to the unions they would work with the existing employees – no one would lose their job. To everyone's surprise, in a couple of years they completely turned around the working culture of the factory, and, without significant investment, the Japanese management structure transformed the worst GM plant into its best – quality-, delivery-, and cost-wise. We were now sold on the idea that culture made the difference to scale-up rather than investment, so were keen to hear the story from one of its key protagonists.

"The secret to Toyota's enduring success," Yoshino-san started, "is that there is no secret. Toyota is a serious company, that is all." We cringed. Not again, we thought. But then we realized he was not being deliberately provocative. He was being earnest. He was framing.

Yoshino-san is an affable, friendly, soft-spoken veteran of the Toyota of the formative years with a notable command of English due to his years spent in the United States. Seriousness meant committing to clear, challenging goals and looking seriously for the most adapted method to reach them. We recognized the same thinking as our sensei's insistence on "clear gains, persuasive logic." By seriousness, he meant attitude towards one's work. His first points will be familiar by now: 1) go and see for yourself to find out the situation firsthand, 2) "no problem is a problem" (welcome adverse information and encourage local problem-solving), and 3) go and look for information yourself rather than wait for the information to be brought to your attention. This, we felt, we were progressing towards. But his fourth point gave us pause: the process is as important as the result.

Process here is to be understood in terms of steps to attain a goal. A good process is one where the steps are clear and repeatable. It doesn't make it an easy process – this is where improvement comes in. For instance, we have a process to take photos of the cars we purchase and display on the site – these photos are hugely important for customers to make up their minds about the purchase they intend to make. Making good photos involves succeeding at a number of steps – which, in turn, involves solving some problems that are different car by car. Standards are not about mindlessly following steps to get an average photo, but about mastering the recurring issues to get good photos consistently.

A good process means a logical sequence of reasonable steps leading to the desired result. A bad process is full of "Hail Mary passes" – steps that will work out if we are massively lucky that day. Being serious, in Yoshino's terms, meant looking for good results from good processes: logical sequences, repeatable actions, sensible scenarios. Unclear assumptions usually mean crossing fingers and relying on the mercy of the gods – who tend to be merciful one day, a few days, but rarely every day.

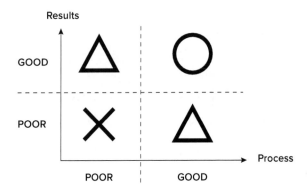

At the value-adding level, such as in the photography booth (to take pictures of cars and then publish them online), it's relatively easy to have an idea of whether we're looking at a good process or a poor one (although, to be exact, when you go into details, it's always harder than you'd think). At the executive level, however, it is very challenging. Most rationales we're given are "just so" stories, nothing more. Very often, executives ask us to arbitrate on decisions where the process to get to the result is unclear – which is one of the reasons their colleagues aren't fully on board and we have to weigh in.

It turns out that insisting on good processes to explain the expected results of executive decisions or proposals is very demanding – it requires seriousness, indeed. Executives argue that there are too many unknowns, too much complexity, and not enough time, all of which is true – but still: how can we wish to be productive at the company level if we're not clearer about the actions we intend to take and why? Furthermore, how can we expect collaboration across functional barriers if specialists can't explain clearly to their colleagues what they're doing and why?

But Yoshino-san did not focus only on process: he also explained that success was the result of pursuing the right kind of results. The role of targets, he argued, was to seek *unconventional* ideas – if not, the business would simply keep on doing what it did. This business of "SMART" (Simple, Measurable, Achievable, Realistic, Time-Limited) objectives was all about keeping people mediocre and the organization uncompetitive. Seemingly impossible targets, on the other hand, are there to spur creativity and develop totally new ideas. He took the example of the original Shinkansen (Japan's high-speed train) development project in the 1960s, which had been defined by framing the project as three key challenges:

- Tokyo to Osaka in three hours
- Achieving a max speed of 250 km/h
- In less than five years

This perfectly scopes the project without prescribing any solution. The lean assumption here is that conventional commands will lead to conventional actions and make you average but not exceptional. Challenging challenges, however, are the key to obtaining unconventional ideas and disrupting the status quo.

Toyota's lean approach to setting targets starts with reflecting deeply about finding the goalpost and then not changing it easily – but changing the means to achieve it. Setting an objective was the outcome of a process by which the currently possible was examined and thoughtfully considered until you saw how to express concrete signposts to define success. One trick is to take the best day of the best month and apply it to each day of the year to see the scope of what is possible. The core idea was that there should be many ways to accomplish one goal.

It's not easy to express complex challenges in terms of concrete goals with visual signposts so people can tell whether they've achieved it or not, whether they're getting closer or drifting further away, and whether their current method will ever allow them to reach the goal. The lesson here is to challenge goals and targets as they're currently expressed and kick them around until you get a fuller understanding of 1) what they really represent and 2) how people interpret them. It's easy to take OKRs at face value and fall down the mental chute of looking how they will be attained without first questioning what challenge they represent and whether the output (the quantifiable result) is an accurate reflection of the outcome (the overall situation you want to reach).

We understood the logic of setting impossible targets, having tried enough crazy gambles in our start-up days (some of which paid up, some of which cost us), and we were constantly frustrated with our managers for not thinking outside the box. We hadn't realized that our very habit of giving out commands and controlling their execution excluded any original thinking. By expressing solutions and not delving into problems, we were setting both the objective and the means, making it hard for anyone to get involved and search for alternate ways of reaching the objectives. It came as a shock to see that the command-and-control style of getting things done was part of the problem of not reaching targets. We needed to learn to clarify the "why?" of goals and open up thinking to the "how?"

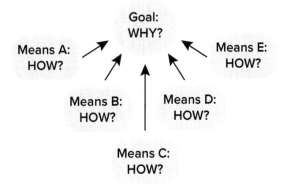

CHAPTER 9:
TEAMWORK TOOLS

I n the late 1970s, Toyota hit a scale-up problem that sounded similar to our present one (at a different scale of course!). The plants had progressed fast, but top management felt that management capabilities and awareness of total quality control were lagging in management functions, particularly away from manufacturing.

In typical Toyota style, they turned to Masao Nemoto (Yoshino-san's first boss), the man who had successfully spearheaded efforts to achieve the Deming Prize in 1965, to come up with a management development program. After going around the company to figure out what the problem was, he concluded that officers were more concerned with finding "who?" than discovering "why?" He wanted to shift the culture from "who made this mistake?" to "what is the cause of this problem?" and consequently focused on sharpening managers' critical-thinking abilities. Isao Yoshino was one of the four-member team that led that program.

The goal of the program, the "what," was to improve four managerial capabilities:

- Planning and judging
- Broad knowledge, experiences, and perspectives
- Driving force to get the job done, leadership, and kaizen
- Presentation, persuasion, and negotiation.

Out of this, Toyota developed a specific tool to address their scale-up issue. Would such a tool work for us?

A3s

At the center of Nemoto-san's management development program was a tool, the "how" – an A3 sheet of blank paper.

Managers went through a presentation session twice per year (June and December). The officers in charge of each department then led question-and-answer sessions with the managers. Officers tried to focus on the problems each manager was facing as well as the effort and process needed to solve the problems. Their aim was to encourage managers to share their problems rather than hide them.

The key to giving the presentations was that they had to be done using an A3 sheet of paper. The managers learned how to select what information/data was needed and what was not needed, since an A3 has only limited space. This helped them select and organize information (the 5S concept as applied to knowledge work). A3 also was a great tool for officers because they could see, at a glance, all the key points that the presenter wanted to convey. As it is just one single document, you can quickly see from the left top corner to the right bottom of an A3 and grasp the key things the writer wants to communicate. This is something that you cannot get from a full written document or Power-Point presentation.

Creating an A3 is essentially a framing exercise: on an A3, you have to put on paper, clearly, how the problem appears to you, what gains you seek, what assumptions you've tested, which cause you're considering first, what strategies you've looked at and which one you've chosen, how you intend to implement the strategy and make sure it works, and so on. This frames the scope of the problem, the nature of the cause (and why we believe it is so), and the kind of solution we consider.

A strong impact the program had on Toyota was to start the "bad news first" culture, which is the entry point to lean thinking. The initial program at Toyota was felt to be successful and was continued to the point that A3, or more to the point *A3 thinking,* became an essential part of Toyota culture.

A3 eventually became formalized in an eight-step pattern Toyota now calls *The Toyota Business Practices:*

TITLE	
1. Clarify the problem	**5. Develop countermeasures**
2. Break down the problem	**6. See countermeasures through**
3. Target-setting	**7. Monitor results and processes**
4. Root-cause analysis	**8. Standardize successful processes**

1. Clarify the problem: Consider the ultimate goal and the current situation, and visualize the gap between current work and the ideal situation.

2. Break down the problem: Break down large problems into smaller, more concrete problems, and clarify quantitatively the point of cause at the gemba to prioritize which problem we will tackle first.

3. Target-setting: Set challenging short-term targets to get to the goal step by step.

4. Root-cause analysis: Thoroughly investigate the process involved in order to clarify the root cause by asking Why? What is actually happening? How do you know that? Why do you think that is?

5. Develop countermeasures: Draw up alternative countermeasures that address the root cause (as many as you can), and evaluate which is the most likely to succeed on a variety of factors such as lead-time, quality, cost, etc.

6. See countermeasures through: Set up the right (visual) reporting so that everyone involved can see progress, and obstacles can be tackled one by one as they appear.

7. Monitor results and processes: Evaluate both the overall results as well as the processes used, and share this evaluation with all involved.

8. Standardize successful processes: Figure out what conditions are needed to make sure the new process will stick, and share the standardized process with other people and divisions.

This is, of course, a highly prescriptive and effective problem-solving approach. But the really important part is that A3 thinking helps senior managers learn to explain the what, how, and why of what they intend to do persuasively, to both engage their staff and involve their counterparts.

For example, Romain, our head of sales, decided to eliminate a mishap liable to impact some of our customers, which turned out to be an issue at our partner financing company.

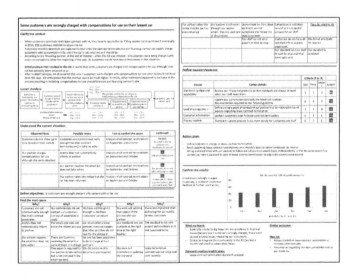

This issue at hand has probably happened to you on the internet. You take a trial subscription to an internet service, then you don't use it and forget about it, only to discover one day as you look at your bank account that the next period has been charged because you didn't properly cancel the contract – and there is no clear and easy way to do so on the site. Some of our customers chose renting with a purchasing option at the end of the rental period. A few of those choosing not to purchase the car were still debited by the finance company – and, rightly, blaming us.

Romain reframed the situation from "sell financing" to "satisfy the customer at the last contact point." He realized that this service worked like many hotels: happy to welcome you in and indifferent to the queue and complications at checkout that have you leaving pissed off. Hotels, he joked, have decided to end every customer's stay with a slap in the face.

He also reframed the relationship needed with the finance partner in order to actually solve singular customer problems and create shared tools to better track real-time customers reaching the end of their lease.

LEARNING TO PITCH

Like most people, at first we thought that these A3s were an exercise in thinking, and we'd ask our execs to present to each other how they were progressing with our A3s, which led to long, unconclusive discussions until the sensei corrected this misconception: A3s are exercises in teamwork, not problem-solving. One first solves the problem and then shares the A3 to share the thinking in storytelling mode. A3s are a structured pitch in a way:

Step 1:	**Why now?** What, in the business context, makes it imperative or relevant to tackle this now?
Step 2:	**Why what?** What part of the problem we've prioritized will we work on first, and why that?
Step 3:	**What gains?** Why is this worth the effort, and what do we expect to gain from it?
Step 4:	**Secret sauce?** Why do we believe this will really address the problem, and have an impact beyond the immediate situation?
Step 5:	**Why how?** Why is the strategy we've chosen better than the alternatives we've considered?
Step 6:	**Next step?** How do we intend to go about it, and who needs to be involved?
Step 7:	**What check?** How do we intend to make sure the effort stays on track and delivers the promised improvement – and question our logic if it doesn't?
Step 8:	**How do we make it stick?** If it works once or twice, what else do we need to change to generalize the change and make it stick?

Reframing A3s this way, we saw that our executives needed to pitch their ideas and plans to each other to gather support. This made us look very differently at change management throughout the company, where one functional leader would initiate a change without letting the others know about it or explaining the potential impact, which was a chaos engine let loose.

In this light, A3s are a powerful teamwork tool that allows our executive committee members to discuss their planned changes and work to help each other across functional barriers rather than constantly deal with the fallout of their decisions and the resulting blame game when implementation runs into the ground.

An Amazon Web Services Executive once told us that Amazon's Jeff Bezos asks his execs to start meetings not with PowerPoint presentations but with six-page narrative Word memos that are read silently at the beginning of the meeting. In an email to his team, Bezos explained: "The reason writing a 'good' four-page memo is harder than 'writing' a 20-page PowerPoint is because the narrative structure of a good memo forces better thought and better understanding of what's more important than what. The great memos are written and rewritten, shared with colleagues who are asked to improve the work, set aside for a couple of days, and then edited again with a fresh mind," wrote Bezos. "The key point here is that you can improve results through the simple act of teaching scope – that a great memo probably should take a week or more."[21]

After a messy period of getting our ideas straight about A3s, executive committee (Excom) members now prepare A3 reports on how they solved problems in their areas and then share these at our weekly Excom meeting. There are eight of us with one A3 weekly, so eight weeks to prepare a report. We went one step further by starting the meeting in customer service to hear the verbatim of one customer complaint, again following Bezos' example, and then have the A3 presentation.

In the ideal A3 presentation, one person would present, each one of the other people in attendance would make one comment, asking for clarification or pushing in another direction, and the rule is that the person pre-

---

[21] R. Umoh (April 23, 2018). "Why Jeff Bezos Makes Amazon Execs Read 6-Page Memos at the Start of Each Meeting," *Make It,* CNBC. https://www.cnbc.com/2018/04/23/what-jeff-bezos-learned-from-requiring-6-page-memos-at-amazon.html

senting *does not answer.* They write the comment down to think about it further – we don't have time for defense and discussion if we want to keep to our schedule during the Excom meetings. Discussion happens out of the room, not during the presentation. We don't always strictly hold to this, but it has done wonders to create *a safe space to speak up.* People know they are expected to come up with something as a proof of listening, and the presenter knows they won't be expected to justify themselves on the spot, just to acknowledge the comment.

It's hard to know if, as the sensei hoped, the A3 presentations made the organization more pliant to change – whether our managers were, in Ohno's terms, more ready to mend their ways. Wrongheaded positions are based on misconceptions and illusions; exploring problems in depth and discussing them with colleagues cleans the window and lets us see how things are more sharply.

What is clear is that we started to reduce our total cost in earnest. Marketing computed that customer acquisition cost was reduced by as much as 30%. Excom members delved into problems with their teams and discovered endless cases of waste. We discovered, for instance, that the majority of users we collected through email list rentals did not turn into customers. We also found out that a costly and complex sponsorship program had zero impact on sales other than to complexify our system and mystify our customers.

In this specific case, Romain was looking for simplification, for either the customers or his team. He believed that the simpler the products, the easier it is to deliver them perfectly with full satisfaction on the customer side. It happens that one of the products Romain's team was managing was a benefit associated with the sponsorship program. By digging into this product, Romain and his team discovered that this perk created confusion for both the salesmen and the customers. Besides, it did not create any value as only 1% of customers were actually using it. Framing these discoveries in an A3 allowed for broader discussion with Guillaume, the head of marketing. Eventually, this resulted in a deeper challenge to assess the value created with the sponsorship program and rethink how we could better engage customers with referrals. Teamwork was happening. It was like looking at two star footballers pass the ball to one another to score a goal.

TURN SYSTEMS INTO REAL ENABLERS TO BUILD A CHAIN OF HELP

"What about your staff?" the sensei asked. "What do you do for them? It's great that you're improving horizontal trust and that functions work better together, but how could we also work on improving vertical trust, within the hierarchical line?" One of our sensei's own sensei, Gilberto Kosaka, a retired general manager from Toyota in Brazil, proposes the following reframe: we must turn the hierarchy from a chain of command to *a chain of help.*

One of the fascinating features of any Toyota plant is their ubiquitous *andon* mechanism. All along the line, a cord runs through that operators can pull if they have a doubt or face a problem. Or buttons they can press at a workstation to ask for clarification: at first doubt on quality or if they see they'll miss the rhythm visualized on the ground, operators pull the cord. This lights up the workstation on a large visible board over the line. As discussed previously, the team leader shows up in less than a minute and either corrects the situation and pulls a second time on the line to restart the line – or not. If he can't fix it immediately, he does not pull the cord a second time, and the line will stop at the next fixed position. The musical alarm gets louder and louder until management rushes in to find out what the problem is.

Two things struck us when we first saw it in action. First, the operator has the concrete power to stop the line. If the issue flagged cannot be resolved within the minute, the line reaches a set spot and ... stops until management fixes the problem. The actual cost to stop an automotive line is not inconsequential, and yet the operator has the power to control the line in that respect. This is awesome.

Second, the operator is never alone with a problem. He pulls the andon cord, the team leader shows up to check whether it's a local understanding or know-how issue, and if he can't fix it right away (pull the andon cord a second time to signal the line to keep running), the line stops and management comes running. The underlying assumption is that every system in the plant is there to work for the operators – to make their job as easy as possible.

This apparently simple tool is revolutionary because it turns on its head two basic assumptions of organizations: hierarchy and Taylorism. Traditionally, bosses make all the decisions; workers execute. Bosses think and tell; workers obey and do. Andon turns this on its head: the operator has to think about her work and spot issues and then has the power to stop the line. Management must then respond to the operator's demand and solve the problem – by doing something. This is a radical change from:

	THINK	DO
Managers	Decide what needs to be done and how to execute the work, and issue instructions.	
Workers		Obey instructions, follow the process, and don't speak up.

To:

	THINK	DO
Managers	Managers clarify challenges, listen to operators input, and frame problems and changes that need to happen.	Go to the workspace and support operators in breaking the pace of work when necessary to create space for investigation and experiments in how to improve the work.

	Look for routine issues in their work and shout out when they see a problem, think about causes, and come up with creative suggestions to solve problems.	Follow standards with care; pull the andon to activate the chain of help at every opportunity; and actively participate in improvement activities to test ideas, evolve standards, and share insights with engineers.
Workers		

This is a radical rethink of how an organization is supposed to work. The implications of both these ideas were quite daunting when we discovered them. We thought back at our own management and systems and, well, to tell the truth, felt quite embarrassed. Because so many of our systems had been cobbled together in our fast-growth period, they were full of holes and discrepancies that frontline staff had to deal with daily. And we didn't see much effort from the management line to help them deal with it – this was quite a wake-up call. If the foundational step of the TPS was indeed "mutual trust between management and workers" and we wanted to build our own version of a lean system, we had to address this head on. How would frontline staff ever trust management if we didn't make more of a visible effort to give them easy-to-work-with systems? How could we get our managers to work *for* our workers – or at the very least with them?

What could we do for frontline staff? Looking at it this way, on the gemba, we realized that employees often struggled with the systems they had to work with. One place to start was to make everyday systems easier to work with.

"How can our systems be true *enablers,*" we asked our executive committee, "rather than a drag on value-adding work?" There was no immediate answer to such a broad question, but the Excom members decided to each look into one system and ask staff: How does this enable you? How does this hinder you? This led us to define an enabling project for each Excom VP, with the aim of making it work.

Enablers are transversal projects – i.e., singular initiatives benefitting both managers and frontline staff – led by one Excom member, with the aim of radically improving day-to-day work conditions for associates. This has led to many breakthroughs. For instance, taking appointments for car deliveries was a headache for many outlets. We set up a pulled flow system that made things a lot easier and led us to be able to deliver a car in 48 hours anywhere in the country. We also helped back-office teams obtain vehicle registration documents with less rework, leading to a twofold increase in productivity. In all these cases, the gains were the result of much-improved teamwork between our front-line staff and their managers.

OBEYA

Drawing from the lessons on the gemba on making work visible, we set up an *obeya* (the Japanese term for "big room") to visualize the various challenges of the executive team.

The obeya of our executive team

This room acts as a control tower for the whole business, visualizing the various irons we currently have in the fire, with:

- *A customer wall:* Pressing, current customer issues that need to be fixed right now

- *A North Star:* Our mission (making car purchase
easy) and vision in terms of challenging goals we want
to achieve as a business

- *Key business indicators:* A wall dedicated to the
key measures we track to have a feel of where the business is and how it is trending

- *Our current battles:* Where we're currently focusing our efforts to reach these goals

- *Enablers:* Where we work on our internal systems
to make them easier to handle for frontline staff

- *Next offers:* The new value we plan to offer customers and how we intend to make it work considering
our present systems

- *Competition:* A part of a wall is dedicated to "how
our competitors are problematic for us"

- *Change plan:* To make sure large functional
changes are communicated ahead of time and people
in other functions ready to adopt them

- *Hoshin kanri:* Yearly strategic plans, function by
function, so the Excom develop a common idea of
where they are taking the company.

Having all these main company KPIs in one single
location creates a cockpit vision of the business that

brings the executive committee together. This clarifies our tactical vision of:

Priorities	What we're trying to do on that front	First thing to learn to succeed

Enabler topics are structured in terms of:

1. Outcome: What we're trying to do in absolute terms

2. Output: What measure we've chosen as the best proxy for the outcome we can think of

3. Past changes: What previous changes we've implemented to get us to where we are

4. Current change: What we're currently trying to do

5. Obstacles and problems: What technical problems we're currently facing (A3s)

6. Next change: What is the next change we're envisioning if we manage to succeed at the current step

The obeya frames change management – quite literally: it gives context to our management discussions on how we handle changes by visualizing the context in which they are discussed. Weekly, we have an executive meeting that starts at the customer service department to hear one specific customer complaint and keep our finger on the pulse of how our customers really experience our service. We then move on to an A3 presentation by an Excom member explaining the change they intend. He or she details the problem they're tackling, the logic behind the change, and how they intend to go about it so that other members of the team can discuss the impact on their systems and areas. Finally, we address whatever pressing tactical issue for which we all need to be on the same page.

Having the key indicators and enabler topics right there in front of our eyes reminds us of what we need to work on together. As a result, we've become far more reactive and responsive – minimizing the potential for issues to fester and grow. Whenever an indicator starts to backslide, we immediately question "why?" and come up with a plan to explore the matter. We're facing our ongoing challenges far more serenely now that people are not expected to deal with issues on their own but can share them with the team.

A SYSTEM TO SUPPORT TEAMWORK
AT ALL LEVELS

Looking into backsliding gave us a renewed appreciation of the need for active teamwork and the power of the *Toyota Production System* as a frame to obtain it. Backsliding happens in the normal course of things, whether in the brick-and-mortar world of logistics or in digital. For instance, our web teams had kaizened out page-loading speed to "top five sites" records, but then backslid – still way better than most sites, but no longer in the top five. Kaizen doesn't happen on its own – we have to be on the gemba to make it happen. As we found out, our first role with the team is to be customer advocates: how can we improve customer satisfaction, either by fixing issues in the current process or by offering new features?

Improve customer satisfaction

To discover the right problems to solve to increase value by simultaneously improving customer satisfaction and reducing total cost, we also learned we had to surface waste and stagnation, through just-in-time lead-time reduction:

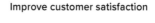

Improve customer satisfaction

Just-in-time:
Reduce lead-
time to
surface
problems

But as you improve quality and reduce lead-time, you also find that things will backslide. Looking into backsliding case by case, we realized that people were reluctant to shout out when they no longer achieved top performance, and that middle management was not ready to jump in and help. The jidoka (intelligent automation) principle of stopping defects and calling them out is necessary to fight backsliding and work your way to more sustainable solutions by tackling issues one by one in real time.

Improve customer satisfaction

Just-in-time:
Reduce lead-
time to
surface
problems

Jidoka: Stop
at every
abnormality,
look into it,
and solve the
problem before
carrying on

To shout out when something is not right, however, requires mutual trust – the foundation step of the TPS. Without the firm shared intention to help each other within teams, across teams, and through the ranks, jidoka remains wishful thinking.

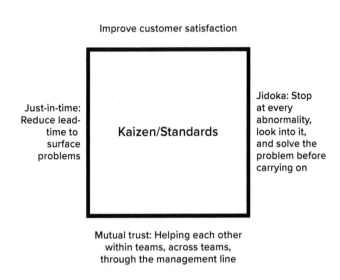

Improve customer satisfaction

Just-in-time: Reduce lead-time to surface problems

Kaizen/Standards

Jidoka: Stop at every abnormality, look into it, and solve the problem before carrying on

Mutual trust: Helping each other within teams, across teams, through the management line

Looking into backsliding showed us, first, that teams surprised us with improvements. However, this required that we spend time on the ground to repeat our challenges and explain what we were trying to do, particularly in terms of just-in-time. Furthermore, performance improvements are hard to maintain as long as deeper systems in the company are not changed as well. To understand these deeper issues, management must look into specific problems and work with other functions to fix them. To have teams practice their own kaizen and maintain their own standards, management – and particularly senior management – must go and see at the workplace with the frame of the TPS resolutely in mind.

Scale has the effect that people no longer see themselves as part of a team – where everyone can talk to everybody else – but frame their work in terms of boss-subordinate relationships. Each person seeing themselves as a link in a chain of command makes it very difficult to develop autonomous problem solvers because, as happened often, when you ask people to look into a problem and think it through – which is essentially a command – they answer with: just tell me what you want, and I'll do it.

Talking to Toyota executives about how the company developed its middle managers, we realized that Toyota didn't send in uber-bosses from Japan to run things – this would not help the plants become self-reliant. What they did was send "coordinators" to support (and train) managers: managers of equivalent level in Japan who had spent time working alongside their Western counterparts to coordinate with headquarters and tell them how issues would be handled in Japan.

These coordinators don't have a hierarchical relationship with the person they support. They're not even properly "coaches." They make no decisions. They are there to show managers Toyota's cultural kaizen way.

Command-and-control is a necessity of scale. Without it, you can't run large bureaucracies. Using kaizen to fight the accumulation of red tape, however, requires a challenge-and-support structure, a different approach to managing people. To do so, however, we learned that the "support" element needs massive amounts of teamwork at all levels. Without it, people respond easily enough to the challenge with kaizen effort, but don't know how to sustain it and exhaust themselves. Developing people is made possible by an environment of safe teamwork.

FIX THE TEAM FIRST

Early in our first experiments with lean, we had been taught about broken processes. The theory was that delivery depended on process performance, and bad processes led to poor delivery – it wasn't a people problem. Spending time on the gemba and challenging operations, we learned that it's all about the people: processes are what people do. Processes depend on the people's shared intention. Some teams want to make the process work and solve problems for customers and each other. Others focus narrowly on each person "doing their job," and results are what they are.

Improving processes sustainably requires that people *first* agree on the problems. For this, people within the process need to understand and trust each other to share issues and get to a consensus on what the problems really are. Problems are the signs of hidden knowledge points, which need to be revealed in order to find robust solutions. To get there, we need visible intent to help each other within teams, across teams, and across hierarchical lines.

For instance, we used to struggle with our financing services – a feature critical to both our customers, who needed it to purchase their cars (and was a serious source of dissatisfaction), and to our profitability. Sales complained of daily outages of the system and blamed IT and the external partner that handled our financing. IT hunkered down and went to work on something else. It was a mess. Romain, head of sales, and Jean-Michel, head of IT, finally sat down together and looked at right-first-time for each customer project – they realized something went wrong in an astounding 30% of cases.

Delving into the details together, case by case, they saw that the main IT process wasn't very intuitive but was robust – a large number of issues came from coding errors on the sales part. The file would go to the partner, then be sent back for correction, then return, and eventually got approved, but at great expense of lead-time, customer annoyance, and wasted effort – plus the creation of bad blood between each of the functions. Focusing specifically on the "over the wall" interfaces, sales and IT nearly eradicated the outages and the rework – a new knowledge point. Now Romain and Jean-Michel have a fortnightly check session to look at case-by-case issues, which they'd never done before. It seems obvious in hindsight, but with an infinite number of things to keep cooking at any one time, keeping a close track of the sales/IT interface on financing had not been spotted before. This new knowledge point enabled us to offer a much better service and lower internal costs.

To foster a growth culture, you need to demonstrate that you are serious about performance improvement; that people will be helped with their improvement initiatives; that they will be listened to when they mention the (unavoidable) backslides and deeper problems;

and that we will, each in our own jobs, work with them to sort one problem after next.

To make this happen, we used tools so that people can share their reasoning and intentions, enabling everyone to see we're actively working on solving systems problems. Regularly, the Excom members make short videos to share their progress on their enablers that we post on our internal social media network. As leaders, we now see that our first priority, before jumping to solutions, is to fix the team: Who should be working with whom on that? Are they? If not, why? And what can we do about it?

Practicing teamwork led us to think differently about management. First, the key to making processes perform is to connect positive-energy people with a common challenge and common methods to come up with the necessary changes to make the process work. Every time this happened, progress has been visible and sometimes spectacular. Second, the chain of command must become a chain of help to support and develop each person in their current role and not hesitate to let them seek their fullest ability. As the sensei asks: why is this person not at the next level? Both of these transformations rest on a foundation of mutual trust, which grows from a sense of shared intent that we all work towards customer satisfaction and that we all will help each other to achieve it. Teamwork, as a verb, means looking for opportunities to work with colleagues within our team or across functional borders to find new solutions to enduring problems.

Working on teams and teamwork was a pivot point – and something of a mental revolution for us. It led us to clarify our management model as a ladder to scale, starting with creating a psychological safe space for "bad news first" and ending with customer loyalty, the true foundation of sustainable growth and profitability:

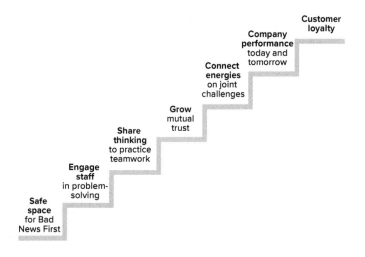

We now could see clearly what we'd be getting wrong, and what our middle managers had never been told – which also gave us a framework to help people grow as managers. Here again, with hindsight, "fix the team" seems banal and something we would have agreed before practicing teamwork in earnest – but the sheer impact of it on performance was mind-blowing and had completely escaped us. We'd been taught to see the organization as a machine, with leaders giving instructions and everyone else applying them. Seeing the company as connected energies that need to be fed and aligned was a radically different vision, and it also shed a different light on all the lean tools we'd learned previously. We also were discovering the lean potential to secure the continuity of customer satisfaction by reconciling different functions – customers with sales outlets, functions with one another, staff with management, the company with its partners. Using framing to practice teamwork as a verb truly made us step in a wider, better room.

CHAPTER 10:
HOW DID
WE GET HERE?

Mid-2017, six months after our early painful (but eye-opening) experiences on the gemba, something was working, although we weren't exactly sure what or how. Our scale-up had been hurting us in stalled sales, diminished customer satisfaction (with a Net Promoter Score at an all-time low in mid-2016), and marketing and overhead costs that grew faster than we could grow turnover. By mid-2018, we were convinced the turnaround was happening. We had started growing again. More importantly, our Net Promoter Score showed steady progress (we also had taken it out of incentive plans to avoid some artificially high scores of the past).

Net Promoter Score (global)

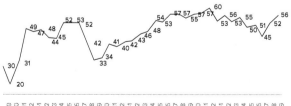

During this time, we also did not spend increasing amounts in customer pacification. Significantly, the structural growth of our marketing and overhead costs was stemmed as we continued to grow turnover. As a result, we doubled our EBITDA.

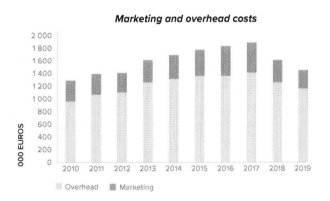

Marketing and overhead costs

What worked?

FOUR STAGES OF A GROWTH MINDSET

We had switched from making decisions and having others apply them to clarifying challenges and encouraging people to solve problems; the sensei suggested we had started to *form* the business, rather than build it. What did that mean? How could we continue to do something that we did not really understand? He considered his job was to teach us gemba lean, which meant progressing through the four following discovery stages at the heart of a growth mindset:

1. Unconscious incompetence: We thought we were doing lean, but we had no idea of what we didn't know – as he'd said on day one, our misconceptions about lean were clouding the window and preventing us from achieving the benefits. Discover that you don't know what you don't know.

2. Conscious incompetence: Realizing that one does not know and committing to learning, which often means changing one's mind and abandoning old ideas, is not an easy challenge to overcome. Discover what you need to learn.

3. Unconscious competence: Things start to work, but we're not quite sure what and why. Performance follows practicing new knowledge points, but it's fragile and prone to backsliding. Practice and experiment with new ideas and actions although they feel very unfamiliar at first. Expect to fail before you succeed.

4. Conscious competence: As unfamiliar practices become more routine, you learn explicit knowledge points and begin to deliberately practice their mastery until they are well known and sustainable. Formalize your understanding of your practice and continue to perfect it. You'll continue to deepen your thinking about what you know and don't know and learn to share it with others.

The sensei felt that we had been experiencing Step 3 – unconscious competence – and had successes without fully understanding what we did right (or wrong). The next step was to better understand the conditions for success we had to create, to become consciously competent about shaping the company for sustainable scale-up. We had learned to find problems, face them, and frame them; we now needed to form the business around adaptive solutions that could only be shared from one person to the next, spilling over rather than being rolled out in cookie-cutter fashion as we were trained.

The traditional way of scaling up a business is to, first, standardize the offer to customers; second, design and set fixed processes using proprietary technology; and third, pressure everyone into complying to the model of using the offered product and finding their place in the process: you optimize the known. And, indeed, this is more or less what we had in mind. This is a tempting route because of the thrill of power and control. You're in charge of your destiny, you're in control of everyone else, and away you go. Although it works in certain circumstances, this approach has four huge drawbacks: it is inflexible in the face of change, it attracts smart jerks, employees are miserable, and it is immensely wasteful.

Serious crises, whether personal or professional, usually start about two years before they are recognized as crises – when the elephant in the room can no longer be ignored. We had a rough patch in 2013–2016, but, looking back, we were struggling since 2010 when we hit the 170 million euros turnover mark (we started our first experiments with lean in 2012 because we felt we had to do *something*). Our strategy hadn't changed – we wanted to create an agile, friendly organization to progressively offer new features to customers to facilitate all aspects of their car purchase. Our intent and the energy we put into achieving the strategy hadn't changed. But we felt the business was resisting us at every turn, and every new feature we offered was polluted by *friction* – a perverse universe thwarting us with small things going wrong everywhere all the time, and people acting mindlessly or politically rather than pursuing their stated objectives.

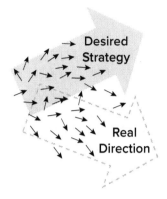

We were solving problems ourselves and making people apply our solutions. Resistance to change is a fancy way of saying no one likes to comply with someone else's ideas. And we expressed these ideas as commands or instructions – no wonder they were easily misunderstood or misrepresented as in our early example of "improve your Google rank."

The about-face the sensei had us do was to go to the workplace and look at the situation from the employee's perspective: in their shoes, through their eyes. What did they see? What did they know? What did they understand? How did they feel about it?

With this in mind, we realized that for all the processes and systems people had to work with, *line of sight* was rarely clear: What did we want to happen?

There was more to it than just how to do the job. Gemba walk after gemba walk, we started realizing this new insight opened up on a radical reframe of strategy:

Set the strategy, find people to execute it, and monitor and control compliance with processes, systems, and tools.

Becomes:

Spell out common challenges, encourage people's insights and initiatives, clarify the line of sight so they themselves can tell how they're doing, and support them with the right enabling tools.

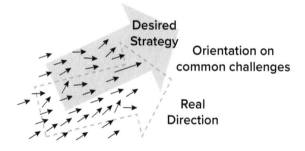

Rather than manage each step of the process and try to control each person's behavior, we could lead them in a clear direction and try to harness their positive energies and creativity. The hard pivot point for us was to learn to express ourselves in terms of problems to be solved as opposed to actions to be implemented.

In production, for instance, when *we* had realized the plant was full of stagnating cars waiting for parts. We then told the purchasing department to purchase parts according to lead-time and forget about price. And yes, this led to a visible improvement in lead-time, which facilitated the spectacular throughput improvement of the plant, which meant we no longer had to build a new facility, so a massive win. But, of course, our parts costs increased as well.

As we returned to visit this team, we explained the trade-off issue – speed of delivery versus best price – to the team leader, who took on the challenge of shortest lead-time whilst reducing overall parts-purchasing costs. This led to a fascinating discussion of priorities with Tanguy, the purchasing team leader – in comparing sourcing outlets, part by part, the faster was not always the most expensive:

	Shortest lead time	Longer lead-time
Best price	Target	?
More expensive	?	No go

As the team explored this, they discovered that their vendors made different calls part by part, and that two other variables came into play: the quantity ordered and the frequency of use:

	Frequent use	One-off
Volume discount	Small inventory	No
No volume price effect	No	No

At first, the team followed our instruction: short lead-time first. But now they faced the trade-off of speed/price and realized that with some high-usage parts they could carry a minimal inventory for some parts with a very high rotation.

We hadn't thought of that. The team figured it out on its own. What had explained the trade-off and given the team space and latitude to experiment with a kaizen methodology. This meant taking a step backwards, and, rather than fixing the *cause* of every issue in the company ourselves, we now saw that we needed to learn to manage the *conditions* in which people could:

• Tackle problems autonomously to better care for customers with increased quality.
• Use tools more smartly to lower total costs.

ORIENT, ENGAGE, INVOLVE

In the sensei's terms, we had to learn to *form* solutions from our people's collective intelligence by *orienting* them in the right direction ("Here's the problem we need to solve, this is the starting point to look into it, and this is the no-go zone we'd like to avoid"); *engaging* them in exploring and trying stuff; and *involving* them in working with other specialists, particularly across functional barriers. A formed solution is not the finished, scalable, on-paper answer to a problem. It's the team that gels around an unexpected insight that they will make work, as Asmaa and Zakaria did with truck appointments or as the marketing team did with SEA.

Creative solutions to thorny problems rarely show up where or when you expect, and, more often than not, someone else has the right insight and needs the help of a specialist to make it work. Back in 2000, Google launched AdWords, an online advertising service based on cookies and key words in which you pay Google to display an ad campaign, placing your copy on search page results. You pay Google on performance – that is, web users who actually click on your ad. Very early on as we were testing the viability of selling cars by phone or on the web, we tried to understand how Google worked because we saw the huge potential of their model for our business. In these early days, we had no contact with the company and would have been way too small to interest them. And, also, to tell the truth, their ad system didn't work so well.

The story is now well known: At some point in 2002, Larry Page got frustrated with the lack of progress with AdWords, printed off a few examples of ads that clearly didn't work with a bold "THESE ADS SUCK" written over them, and on a Friday afternoon posted them on a bulletin board in the office kitchen. The following Monday, a search engineer – who had not been working on anything related to ads – and a few colleagues emailed a detailed analysis of *why* these ads sucked, including a link to a prototype solution the *ad hoc* team had coded over the weekend. The core insight was that Google should compute an "ad relevance score" that would assess the ads' relevance to the query and use the score to determine where to place the ad on the page. The reframe here was to combine the relevance to users with how much the advertiser was willing to pay. Making it work, however, required a lot of high-level computing skill. The rest, as they say, is history, as AdWords became the foundation of a multibillion-dollar business.

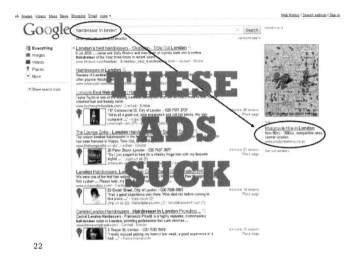

22

The story illustrates what a *formed* solution is. It starts with a *visual* expression of the problem: this leads someone (whose job it wasn't and who had plenty of his own work waiting on his desk) to get *engaged* in the problem and investigate it (through the night, actually), hit upon a new insight, and then *involve* a team of colleagues (over the weekend, nonetheless) to come up with a prototype of what the solution could look like.

In truth, this is what we did routinely back when we were a start-up, and that disappeared when we grew up to become a normal company. To be fair, the "THESE

22 Breckler, A. (Feb. 28, 2016). "These Ads Suck," Medium.com.
   https://medium.com/@adambreckler/these-ads-suck-4892761ea4cb

ADS SUCK" story attracted so much attention because Google hit the jackpot with it. This won't be the case with most problems the business needs to solve. But the radical rethink is to think in terms of problems that need to be solved rather than processes to be maintained. And in any business, there are some problems that will always need to be solved, no matter how good your existing process is.

For instance, our Google friends are notoriously close-mouthed about how their ranking algorithm works. However, they've consistently told us that page-loading time is the No. 1 factor. This is consistent with research that shows that over one second, many users will simply have browsed on. Amazon says that a page-load slowdown of just one second could cost it $1.6 billion in sales each year. Google estimates that by slowing its search results by just four tenths of a second, they could lose 8 million searches per day – meaning they'd serve up millions fewer online ads.[23] No matter how you look at it, page-loading speed is a problem.

[23] K. Eaton (March 15, 2012). "How One Second Could Cost Google $1.6 Billion in Sales," *Fast Company*. https://www.fastcompany.com/1825005/how-one-second-could-cost-amazon-16-billion-sales

Humans, however, habituate. We get used to low-intensity annoyances over a period of time, like living in a noisy apartment: it takes its toll, but you're no longer aware of it. We knew that speed-loading rate had a dramatic impact on conversion rates. We had studies showing how dramatic the effect could be:

Page-loading speed and conversion rate

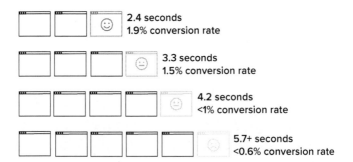

But we had learned to live with it.

In the course of our gemba walks, the sensei had us try another exercise. The problem-solving board at a team level was about engagement, he explained – getting people interested in problem-solving and enthusiastic about being able to find and share countermeasures. We also needed to work on involvement – team efforts to improve current ways of working. To support this, we dedicated another whiteboard to a kaizen six-step method:

Six-step kaizen method

WHAT	HOW
1. Improvement opportunity	What clear gain are we after – why is it a problem, and what concrete gains do we seek?
2. Analysis of current method	Visualization of the sequence of steps of how the process currently works, quantifying the performance at each step to identify the point of cause: the specific point where things go wrong.
3. New idea	A new insight into the problem, a new way to frame it, a new hunch to test.
4. Test plan	Who do we need to convince and involve, and what tests do we need to show them in order to garner support for our new way of doing things?
5. Implementation plan	How do we intend to progress from proof of concept to actual change – what else does it involve?
6. Evaluation and standardization	Did we get the results we expected? Was it really a good idea, or just an idea? If it was a good idea, what else do we need to change in the company for the new way of working to become the new standard?

During a gemba walk, we ended up discussing the loading-speed problem, and the team in charge of the website felt it could try the framework – suck it and see.

Their first discovery was that no one was on the case. To be fair, the SEO (search engine optimization) team was asking for speed, but beyond that everyone felt that as long as features worked, it was OK. Once they started looking into it, they discovered that they didn't know how to achieve speed improvements. They had lost track of technology advances in a fast and furious field, and no one on the team had helped develop high-speed websites.

They started by visualizing the problem in terms of:

• **Performance:** Visualize our performance (speed, but also NPS as a top performance indicator) on a daily basis to verify the results of our actions and to create a fighting spirit on the team.

• **Problems:** Visualize problems by going deep into every asset loaded on every page and look into every one of them, one at a time, with a systematic deep-dive on client roadblocks.

This led to getting closer to our Google partners to build a web performance audit by Mobile Specialist in June 2018; a list of potential optimizations; regular follow-up calls and Q&As with our technical team covering tech deep-dives, processes, and tooling advice;

and delivery of a mobile usability audit (UX) audit in November 2018 to help us assess the gap. This, in turn, encouraged them to test new ideas to improve the way objects on the web page were rendered (image management and prerendering of assets) and optimize the technical infrastructure to reach the highest standards in the industry.

As a result, the load time of the homepage went from 10.4 seconds to 3.7 seconds on mobile, mobile conversions increased by 22%, and bounce rate (the percentage of visitors who navigate away from the site after viewing only one page) decreased by 16%. Our speed index also improved, with mobile conversions now as high as desktop ones – which also meant up to four places gained on some SEO searches. Google now tells us that we're one of the fastest sites they work with – but that's not the point. The point is that page-loading speed will never not be a problem.

The kaizen method turned out to be the key to forming solutions within the team, just as A3 did in the executive committee. But it required a radical shift of focus. Looking at process and ensuring they ran OK was not enough. We also needed to think in terms of typical problems of the business and then wonder which delivery processes sustained them. The new knowledge point for us was to start listing such typical problems as page-loading speed.

Delivery process	Process A	Process B	Process C	Process D
Typical problem				
Problem 1	•			•
Problem 2		•		
Problem 3		•	•	
Problem 4	•			•

From that, we sought to understand how typical problems and delivery processes interacted. We have many such problems that we can pick up from our gemba visits. For instance, customer welcome never ceases to be a problem, and so is helping customers with switching options (finding the car that best fits their budget and usage, and one that we can procure instead of the one they first had in mind), pricing cars, etc. In procurement, a steady supply of exciting models also will never cease to be a problem and so on. Cyril, our lean program director, is currently in charge of redefining the program in terms of typical problems throughout the business.

Over time, our scale-up model has switched from the usual one (standardize the offer, implement processes, pressure on compliance) to an alternative one that hinges on three skills:

• First, discover and formulate "typical problems," such as the page-loading speed problem, the quick-car-delivery problem, or the making-every-person-feel-welcome problem – impactful problems that will always be there no matter how good we get at solving them, where backsliding is always a risk, and where staff will unavoidably habituate to less-than-perfect results.

• Once we have a clearer handle on these essential typical problems, the second skill is developing a culture of problem-solving. This involves encouraging a *growth mindset* belief in the possibility and usefulness of learning as well as teaching a consistent method for problem-solving – what, in medicine, is called problem-based learning. By training everyone in standard problem-solving tools, we can connect high-energy people to solve problems together and foster a culture of autonomy in problem-solving.

• Finally, as senior management, we can commit to offer our staff ever more enabling tools to do their jobs easily and well and to build the results of their kaizen improvements into the systems of the company.

The challenge was that staff throughout all levels of the company require different tools and levels of support. How could we deliver?

CHAPTER 11:
ENCOURAGE INITIATIVE AT ALL LEVELS

We had a better grasp of what we wanted to do (shift from a traditional scale-up to a lean scale-up), and now we needed to clarify how to do it in order to continue to make progress over the coming years.

TRADITIONAL SCALE-UP	LEAN SCALE-UP
Select customers satisfied with standardized offers. Acquire best practice and invest in rigorous process. Pressure customers, employees, and suppliers to comply to processes. Satisfy people who best fit the role with pay-for-performance.	Develop a culture of problem solvers to respond flexibly to customers by clarifying challenges and visualizing problems. Look for high-energy people to engage and involve in finding and solving problems together. Support them with enabling tools and appreciation.

The change of perspective the sensei kept insisting on was to look at the situation from the people on the ground's eyes: what did they need to work well and feel they contributed through suggestions and ideas?

Our experience with framing led us to believe that the company needed to provide to a person doing the frontline work:

1. A clear sense of purpose: Frontline workers want to see their individual impact on meaningful work with clear goals and work tools and with a clear *line of sight* to the overall mission (what we're here to do), vision (what we'd like to achieve), and challenges (what are the obstacles facing us).

2. A safe and interesting workplace: We needed to create a balance of routine work with interesting projects in open and dependable teams where everyone knows what they're doing.

3. An enabling work environment: Individuals require functional support and working tools that enable them to do their job well as well as a development path through the company supported by senior-management interest and mentoring.

To form solutions across the organization, we looked at the company structure, and we felt we could intervene at four levels: founders and leaders (us), department heads in charge of specific functions, frontline/middle managers in charge of several teams, and team leaders in charge of value-adding teams.

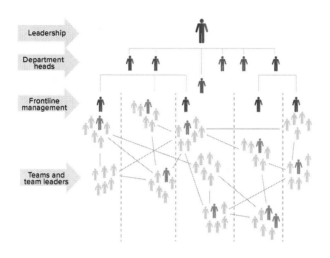

LEVEL	WHAT	HOW	TOOLS
Team leaders	• Psychological safety and job challenge • Day-to-day running of the team in an open manner with a good atmosphere • Space to think and experiment	• Show respect • One-to-one conversations to clarify priorities • One-to-one coaching • Managing team mood • Helping with day-to-day problems and team challenges	• Treating people as individuals • Listening skills and courtesies • Visual management of team metrics • Coaching to standards • Making everyone participate in problem-solving sessions • Team kaizen activities
Frontline/middle managers	Coaching and support on everyday problems	• Chain of help	• Andon and kanban

Depart-ment heads	• Enabling processes and a support on progress in the organi-zation • Coordi-nation with other functio-nal heads to solve critical problems • Support for staffers ta-king initiative	• Practice teamwork • Solve pro-blems across functional barriers • Encourage inventive initiatives • Support with mento-ring • Access to training and tools	• Company obeya • A3 presenta-tions • Enablers and department
Founders and leaders	• Line of sight • Customer orientation • Clear challenges • Visual pro-blems • Attention, encourage-ment, and approbation to sugges-tions	• Go and see • Problem-fin-ding during gemba walks • Coaching to visualize performance and problems better • Give exer-cises • Storytelling to explain why it mat-ters	• Gemba walks • Visualization techniques • Typical pro-blems • Storytelling

We recognized that to create the conditions that enable people to orient themselves towards customer value and company challenges, we had to delve into problems and connect with each other to come up with innovative solutions. We could start with practicing a few everyday skills at each level of the organization – and helping our people with acquiring these skills.

TEAM LEADERS: SHOW RESPECT TO SUPPORT GROWTH-MINDSET TEAMS

What conditions do people need to learn and to discover new ideas? Looking into all the cases of new insights, we narrowed it down to two prerequisites:

- A recognizable, repeated problem
- A belief that learning is possible and worthwhile

To learn as an organization, we need to structure the workplace as discrete learning curves: for each new, discovered knowledge point. We need to structure a learning experience, and this hinges on the team leader's ability to:

- Maintain visual management to physically create a recognizable, repeated problem that people can learn to tackle better.
- Share their conviction that self-development through learning is the norm: it is achievable and worthwhile for the company, and the effort is worth it for the person.

It seems obvious with hindsight, but the *team leader* is key to learning day to day. In fact, if we intend to develop a team of teams, it should be hardly surprising. But like many truths staring at us right in the face, this is easy to miss – there are too many team leaders to keep track of them personally, and the management of team leaders is often delegated to HR and the department heads. When you visit team after team, you can see for yourself the impact the team leader has on whether the team develops a growth culture or a fixed culture – it matters far more locally than our efforts at the company level.

If we look at it from the associate's perspective, people demand three things of a team leader: 1) a sense of belonging to a good team, both trustworthy and competent; 2) learning technical skills and personal support on next steps; and 3) sorting out occasional problems, with the organization and personal issues, with fairness. Being a good team leader of five to 10 people calls for social skills as well as technical competence. To help our team leaders get a better grasp of the job, we support them with four basic tools:

• **Visual management and daily management** are the keys to regular, individual conversations about priorities. Probably the most effective team-leadership technique is a weekly one-to-one with each person to discuss priorities in the present context. "What are your priorities? How can I support you?" Simply discussing where people are at, the obstacles they see, and how they intend to go about them is the founding rock of team leadership. In this, maintaining the visual management of the workplace is very helpful because it gives context to priorities. The simplest tool is a whiteboard detailing the day's success. A more sophisticated tool is a kanban to sequence work. In any case, clear performance metrics and visual processes frame the conversations and make them easier to have. Be it as it may, tool or not, the key skill here is listening and asking "why?" People need to feel considered as individuals and absolutely need a say in their priorities to be engaged in their work.

• **Dojos** create a specific time and place to look into the detail of work and existing standards. A "dojo" is a room or a hall in which martial arts are practiced. In lean, a dojo is individualized training where the team leader spends 20 minutes with team members to see how the person handles routine situations and to coach them. Standards, which are documented sequences of steps clarifying the knowledge points, are a useful tool to support the team leader in her coaching. We recommend that team leaders set aside 20 minutes every day to spend time on individualized coaching in order to help people master the basics of the job and seek more edgy knowledge on problematic configurations. A key insight from our early gemba walks was that our systems were often so complex people simply did not know how to use them and worked around them. With dojos, we can clarify knowledge points and pick specific areas for improvement.

- *Problem-solving boards* visualize a standard problem-solving process and support participation. At the problem-solving blackboard, either the team leader or an associate presents to the team a *solved* problem. This is the starting point of a conversation where the team leader must learn to include everybody: everyone has a say, everyone has a go. The aim is to grow the team's sense of connection and safety – everyone is expecting to share their opinion, and no one will make fun of them or put them down. Great team leaders have the knack of supporting high-energy, quick, inclusive conversations that make the team come together and grow its belief that by trying one thing after another, most problems can be solved – the key entry ticket to a growth culture. The team must believe that they're in this together, that everyone is pulling their weight, and that learning time leads to success.

- **Six-step kaizen boards** support the storytelling about improvement work and clarify the logic of forming improvements (as opposed to jumping to solutions). Doing good routine work and solving daily problems is not enough to keep teams interested in their jobs and focused on performance. We must also provide them with space to think where all the answers are not yet known and it's not a question of applying one best practice or other, but of discovering for oneself better ways to work. The team leader can be helped by the kaizen office specialists, but the key skill lies in giving clues and hints to keep the group going – but NO ANSWERS. People on the team must think, think, think.

Kaizen, for a frontline team, rests as much on motivation as analysis. These "thinking spaces" are essential to create safe spaces where everyone's opinion is valued and taken into account. If the team leader uses the problem-solving board or the six-step kaizen board to think out loud and tell the team what he wants to happen, in proper command-and-control mode, the benefit of the tools is lost – plain and simple. The boards are designed to create a space for voluntary participation. We need to train the team leader to use this space in that way, to draw every person in, and to encourage participation – often not an easy challenge.

FRONTLINE/MIDDLE MANAGERS: THE CHAIN OF HELP

In a traditional command-and-control structure, the middle managers' role is mainly about compliance, reporting, and handling people issues. Compliance is tricky, because middle managers are expected to simultaneously get people to follow the company's procedures and processes while also implementing changes driven by the top – both instructions being often contradictory. Managers also are expected to keep up the reporting that feeds the department head's demands for information. And managers also need to deal with all the personal crises that come up in the course of work. As we discussed, individuals' dissatisfaction tends to crystalize on unexpected issues, which they then will negotiate with ... their manager. Middle managers deal with one people issue after the next, never quite sure which fire will suddenly flare up – fires which they can deal with either in authoritarian or problem-solving ways.

The gemba lean approach challenges established middle-management roles because, first, the CEO and top leaders now go to the workplace rather than solely relying on reporting – they talk directly to team leaders and team members about local conditions, which can put the middle manager on the spot. Second, middle managers are now expected to adapt processes to integrate the results of kaizen activities – this means handling change from the ground rather than from the top. Third, in lean, middle managers are expected to look at people's progress in the organization, rather than convince them to stay forever in the same job.

Turning the chain of command into a chain of help will succeed or fail at the middle-management level, and we have to recognize how much of an orientation change this really is.

The key lean tools of middle managers are andon, visual standards, and team motivation.

The most powerful of these is andon: a visual signal triggered by the operator to shout out that something isn't right. A team leader jumps in and helps figure out what the problem is and whether it can be sorted out right away, by pointing towards the right standard. If this cannot be done, the team leaders flag the frontline manager, and, with the team member, they examine the deeper issue. Andon is the key to turning the chain of command into a chain of help, but we've also found it difficult to set up in practice. Here you see an andon signal for our customer service staff for when a call gets tricky.

Andon signal (light) for our customer service staff

Andon is about distinguishing the familiar and predictable from the unpredictable. It is NOT about taking over from the team member, who still owns the job, but about preventing anyone from facing a problem alone. Management is supposed to help, not hinder. And help comes in the form of standards, the second key tool for frontline management. Standards are not procedures, but the sequence of knowledge points one has to master to do a job well. Operators are supposed to master knowledge points about predictable calls. Managers are expected to be familiar with knowledge points on how to deal with less predictable situations.

The most predictable standards, ideally, should be built into the environment visually so that normal is easily distinguished from abnormal. The maintenance of this visual environment and the detection of abnormalities are the core jobs of middle management in a lean culture.

The third fundamental aspect of lean middle management is maintaining team motivation as opposed to the individual compliance of traditional command-and-control instruction. Team motivation is the secret sauce to well-performing processes and to the shared intention to maintain standards, as opposed to cut corners. Lean rituals such as 5S and daily huddles are meant to build motivation, but if misinterpreted can just as well create demotivation. It is essential for us as leaders to convey to our frontline management that team motivation stems, first, from approval and fairness in addition to a safe and clean workspace. Approval is easy when everything goes right, but that's rarely the case. Disapproval comes naturally in case of any problem – we have to train ourselves to approve that a problem was revealed.

Kaizen initiatives are a great vector for approval – the manager can approve the team for their effort, whether the kaizen is ultimately successful or not. A turning point in lean thinking is the pivot from

Job = Work
to
Job = Work (with standards) + Kaizen

Middle managers who make the pivot to lean thinking, first, look at everyone's contribution to quality as a dedication to mastering the *standards* in their daily jobs; only through standards can high quality be guaranteed. Then managers come up with insights and *suggest* initiatives to improve standards in unusual situations or in an attempt to eliminate obvious waste.

Finally, in involving oneself in team kaizen efforts, managers continuously review work processes, find improvement opportunities, test them, get them approved, and then change the underlying procedures to improve the way we work collectively.

A common problem we face with secondhand cars is keyed-cars vandalism: doors or bonnets with key scratch marks. To try to remove scratches, our team members follow the procedure recommended by the scratch removal liquid supplier:

1. Sand to remove the varnish (remove the scratch as much as possible without touching the base, and the V formed during the scratch is reduced as much as possible); sanding must be gradual with three different grains.
2. Polishing with various products:
    a. First buffing with the green container, which contains microbeads, to erase the traces of sanding
    b. Second buffing with the yellow can for shine
    c. Third buffing with the blue can to remove the holographic effect

Our most experienced polisher, Benjamin, thought about how the polishing product affected the varnish on the car door and started buffing intensely with the product to fill the scratch with microbeads before sanding:

1. Intensive polishing with the green canister to fill the scratch with the microbeads.

2. Once the two edges meet, go to the sanding step to put everything at the same level (we keep the three grains, but we do a lighter sanding).

3. Polishing:
   a. Green can (erases sanding marks)
   b. Yellow can for shine
   c. Blue to remove the hologram effect

By filling in the gap first, he is able to make deeper scratches disappear – which saves us from either ordering a new part or displaying the scratch so that customers know what they are buying. The kaizen idea leads to a new standard and so on. Such a "small" improvement might sound trivial, but Benjamin's improvement reduces scratch polishing from two to three hours to close to 20 minutes. Considering that about 50% of cars going through bodywork have scratches on them, this has a visible impact on throughput. But, more importantly, this is truly innovative thinking from Benjamin, which then spreads to his team and all teams.

Nicolas trying out Benjamin's new polishing approach

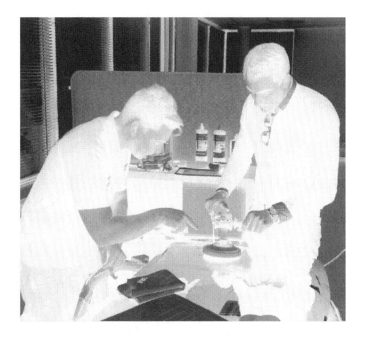

Our epiphany was twofold. First, we see the company not as a sum of instructions to be applied by workers, but as an accumulation of creative ideas that support each other like a mountain cairn. The second realization is that frontline managers and middle managers are the key to this transformation. Benjamin would never have followed through on his idea without the interest and support of Fred, the production manager, and Remi, the plant leader. Middle managers need to understand how profoundly their support of workers affects the company and practice it by encouraging a kaizen-first attitude (do the kaizen now to improve daily work, rather than wait for all work to be finished to look into kaizen). This means working day after day at keeping up the problems-first attitude that creates the foundation for people to point out waste and feel supported in trying new things to eliminate it.

DEPARTMENT HEADS: PRACTICE TEAMWORK TO CREATE AN ENABLING ORGANIZATION

Department heads have a crucial role in forming solutions. They either enable people to pursue their intuitions – with time, tools, and encouragement – or they can stifle them. In the Google AdWords story, imagine that the engineer who cracked the problem had his boss constantly reminding him of his own work piling up on his desk and frowning on any initiative that didn't pursue direct departmental objectives. "These ads suck" would have remained an irritated note from the boss on a billboard; the story *would never have happened.*

Functions have their own culture, and the department head is usually incentivized on functional objectives. He naturally considers that all work in his department should go towards his achieving the objectives he's committed to. This makes sense, but the downside of this is an extractive outlook on the business: seeing the company as resources to achieve one's objectives regardless of any other outcome and mining the company for it – often at the expense of other departments.

Department heads have an essential role in, first, reframing who their users are. It's easy to see how the finance director considers that his users are the external auditors and the shareholders. We count on him to see that his users are our team leaders that need to have a clear sense of how the business is doing to develop their own judgment on financial matters. Clarifying who users are to their own department staff makes a huge difference to how teams see their jobs.

The second step that department heads can take to help create better conditions to form solutions is to actively practice A3s and share them. Clarifying goals and learning to write more persuasive logic spreads the feeling of togetherness across the company and helps people in other specialties understand the key issues even if they don't fully grasp the technicalities of the countermeasures. Framing issues makes them easier to share across functional borders and build the sense of collective destiny in the plant. By writing a first A3 on how customers were charged incorrectly by the finance partner, the head of our commercial network got the head of marketing thinking and working on the project and coming up with a solution. Most problems initiate far in time and place from where the symptom appears, and sharing A3s is key to tracing problems to their root cause and where they originate in the organization.

A3s are also a good tool to clarify departmental priorities. The department head can write a yearly A3, which is then reviewed in mid-year, expressing challenges, results of the previous year, problems to solve in the current year, and learning from the process. Here is the commercial VP's plan for his area.

Commercial department annual plan

Hoshin Kanri : Sales Department — Date : nov. 2019

Vision : Offer a seamless, pro&friendly multi-channel shopping experience to facilitate decision-making for our customers, while being the best car sales school in France and a management training school for our employees

Combats
- 1 in 2 customers trust us for financing
- Buy from Aix, optimize budget
- Promoter customers one year after purchase
- In less than 90 min : safe, recovery, financing
- 95% of customers find an answer on Aix.com
- Talent and teamwork to win

Fights	Feedbacks FY18	Challenges for FY19	Target	Problems to track	Timing	Status

These A3s are shared within the department in a catchball[24] process to create consensus on achievable goals. Then they're shared across department heads to create a unity of purpose in what each sector is doing.

A third step to solution-forming for department heads is to visibly reduce interdepartmental meetings, instead sharing out talented staff with other departments. One thing that cogs up companies as they grow are the endless middle-management meetings where everything is discussed and nothing is decided (mostly to get people on the same page).

Fourth, department heads also can support workers actively by taking an interest and encouraging kaizen in their teams. Kaizen needs time, space to think, and – especially for the fourth step (test plan) and sixth step (standardization) – coordination with existing processes to make the solution stick. A kaizen idea is like a seedling that needs careful protection and watering to grow into a full-blown solution. Department heads are the gardeners. They can either let kaizen ideas wither or help them bloom.

---

[24] Catchball involves moving ideas and information from one person or team to another, much like the game of catch where children throw a ball to each other.

FOUNDERS AND LEADERS: GO AND SEE TO DISCOVER PROBLEMS AND VISUALIZE LINE OF SIGHT

As we've seen throughout the book, the CEO's most impactful presence is, strangely, not in the boardroom, but on the frontline. Certainly, there are some hugely impactful decisions only a CEO can take, such as acquire a company, start a new line of business, invest in an expensive new tech, or hire a vice president. But the day-to-day reality of the boardroom is a string of meaningless reports and presiding over bitter turf battles where one has, to tell the truth, not much real bearing.

On the frontline, on the contrary, CEOs can have a unique impact that doesn't require being there long or often: they can contribute to a growth culture by reinforcing "high-road" thinking; giving a sense of a positive future; showing which challenges the company still needs to face to fully satisfy customers; reinforcing belonging by showing interest and appreciation in individuals' skills; and getting interested in details, not with the aim of intervening but to discover the realities of work at the source and to encourage teams in creating space to think about their work.

The first tool of the leader is the plan of gemba visits: the team knows the CEO is coming and will visit several teams every week. A clear plan lets everyone know what is going on and when they're expected to have a kaizen to show. In gemba walks, the CEO will focus on visualizing performance and processes to reveal problems: he or she is in a unique position to teach visualization because he understands like no one else the need for line of sight – orientation – needed for each team to succeed as a company beyond functional perspectives.

Asking *"why?"* and being geeky and patient when conversations get technical is an essential part of frontline management. As we've seen throughout the book, many solutions were born from a detailed technical insight, often poorly phrased and poorly hatched. Staying patient and keeping focused as conversations get deeply technical has a disproportionate impact on the team by encouraging them to get to the bottom of problems and look for smart countermeasures.

Gemba visits must lead to promoting growth-mindset leaders. A classic bias of large companies is to think they don't have enough talent inside, and so they look to headhunters to find experienced professionals to fill the job. As we now learned the hard way, this often means bringing in fixed-mindset professionals whose main priority is taking care of their résumés and preparing for their next job in four years. By spending time on the gemba, the CEO learns to recognize problem-solving talent in less-showy people and to promote leaders that somehow combine a curiosity about the job with a way to make teams come together.

FORMING SOLUTIONS ACROSS ALL LEVELS

A solution is born when someone reframes an old problem and comes up with a new angle to attack it. But even if it's put on paper, it isn't *real*. The solution has no existence beyond the head of the person who's had it and out of the heart that will lead to something concrete.

In today's organization, few ideas can be fully realized just on one's own. The next step for the idea to become a solution is for the person to find the right allies to build a prototype to see if the idea works. From one person's head, the idea now lives in a few – and they're the ones who will turn it into something concrete that can persuade others.

Kodak invented digital photography – and then its decision makers chose not to pursue it for fear of endangering its leading cash-cow products (film). We're all Kodak. Once an idea is born, it has to fight layers of middle management for the right to continue and thrive, to emerge. We hold on to the myth that solutions are built: someone solves the problem, others execute it, then create the process to scale it, and so it goes. That's simply not how it goes. Ideas grow from intuitions and then evolve with conversations and bits of code until some workable prototype is on the table. Solutions are *formed* by people with people – not built by a regimented process. Creativity is … creativity. It needs space to thrive.

Most of the solutions that came out of our efforts to create a growth culture came out of the same sequence of uncontrollable events. Someone finds a problem. A leader faces it ("These ads suck"). Someone else gets to thinking about it and reframes the problem – and then goes on to enlist allies to form a solution. Careless executives kill it.

The hard truth to face is that the limits to our growth were imposed by the creativity and initiative of our people, which our command-and-control structure had been thwarting at every point. We understood we needed to let go of trying to control every cause and instead create the conditions for inventiveness, *at every level of the company.*

The new knowledge points we had now to figure out is how to inspire people to reframe issues and form new solutions. This was the linchpin of our emerging scale-up model, and, as the sensei had maintained from the start, it was as much a question of motivation as a matter of thoughtful analysis. We needed to get better at creating space to think and orienting, engaging, and involving everyone on our teams. But for this to work, we needed to adopt a radically different perspective on strategy.

CHAPTER 12:
RAISE THE BAR

All around us, the business world – investors first of all – seems to evaluate leaders along the two dimensions of strategic insight and clarity and then execution capability. We now see that this doesn't make any sense. Both are intimately linked: strategy insight and clarity come from deeply understanding execution problems, and delivery hinges on taking on the right strategic problems in the first place.

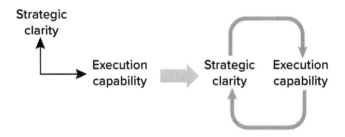

Our perspective has changed to one with a deeper sense of what makes success, moving from:

We are sole masters of our fate, we come up with plans and find people to execute it, and then they are realized to the extent of favorable or unfavorable circumstances.

to:

We are challenged by events and external forces, share these challenges with our allies to come up with a response, and study and improve that response while understanding that our success goes through their success.

As we progressed in clarifying the conscious competence of how we were leading the company with lean, we were also deepening our understanding of lean's strategic impact – and finding that our learning path paralleled that of other lean leaders.

"Fix the base, grow the business," Orry drew on the whiteboard. Orry Fiume is the retired chief financial officer of Wiremold, one of the most famous lean success stories that largely contributed to defining "lean" in the 1990s (and one of the cases in the seminal book *Lean Thinking*[25]). Art Byrne, the CEO, and his management team grew the company's value by 2,467% in 10 years:

[25] J. Womack & D. Jones (1996). *Lean Thinking,* Simon & Schuster, New York

sales more than quadrupled, gross profit jumped from 38% to 51%, inventory turns increased from 3X to 18X, and EBITDA progressed from 6.2% to 20.8% – a spectacular success story by any account. Orry cofounded the lean accounting movement and frequently writes about lean as *strategy*.[26] We met Orry at a lean summit and were keen to have him come in to give his perspective on how we were going about lean because we seldom come across lean experts with a *business* outlook. Orry, a serene-looking, white-haired, soft-spoken man with an amused and curious twinkle in his eye got the conversation going by asking us, "What do you want to be when you grow up?" He then patiently listened to how what we were *doing now* would lead us *there*.

Wiremold, he explained, had from the start of Byrne's tenure set itself the goal of doubling in size every three to five years, half organically, half through acquisitions. They actually doubled in size the first four years, again in the next four years, and were on their way to doing so again when the family owners decided to sell the company. Since the electrical products industry the company was in grew very slowly, Wiremold could grow in only three ways: take market share

[26] M. Ballé, D. Jones, J. Chaize, & O. Fiume (2017). *The Lean Strategy*, McGraw Hill, New York.

away from competitors (difficult and costly), grow the market itself through new product introductions, or acquire companies with a good strategic fit, whose product portfolio would complement Wiremold's existing offering for its customers.

This was a language we understood, as we were in the process of acquiring a large business to grow our reach in Europe and, let's face it, had not been very successful with our initial attempt of international expansion. Our first venture in organic growth in Germany didn't go well, so we decided to go the acquisition route. We first purchased a start-up in Spain, and then we were in the midst of acquiring a fully grown-up company in Belgium.

FIX THE BASE

The first trick to successful growth, Orry told us, is that the base business first has to work autonomously, which means improving daily through kaizen. Without that, the firefighting necessary to keep the business afloat drains all energies and resources so that the new business, be it product or acquisition, is treated without special care, like additional blocks in the organizational chart – and therefore doomed to fail. To keep the base progressing, we can understand that established business lines fill a niche and don't often have massive space for endless financial growth. However, one can focus on challenging operational stretch goals.

In Wiremold, this meant aiming for:
- 100% on-time delivery
- 50% annual reduction in defects
- 20X inventory turns
- 20% annual productivity gains
- Visual control and 5S
- 20% profit sharing

Orry Fiume, retired chief financial officer

The second trick is to reach these goals through kaizen – teaching teams analysis tools so that they can work on the typical problems that are specific to the business in which the company operates.

In Wiremold, for instance, single-minute exchange of die (SMED) was a key lean tool that taught operations teams to be more flexible and deliver better while reducing inventory. Quality function deployment (QFD) was the key tool Wiremold used to accelerate introducing new products to its markets, and so on.

In the Toyota factories we visited, employee footsteps were always a problem since the layout changes with every model change or line-speed change. For 40 years, team leaders have been taught *standardized work* – the analysis of movement in the cell – to generate kaizen ideas to keep steps to a minimum with the mantra of "one step, one second, one cent." Layout will never not be a productivity problem on a production line.

To fix the base, Orry suggested, we needed to understand the few typical problems that were key to our business performance, codify analysis tools to help the teams, and keep encouraging and supporting kaizen efforts.

The third element to fix the base, he said, was the profit-sharing scheme that ensured that every employee concretely saw the fruits of their efforts. Wiremold already had a profit-sharing plan that was developed by the company's founder in 1916. It was calculated based on quarterly profits and paid in cash to every employee as a percentage of their straight-time pay. Orry insisted that allowing everyone to share financially in the success of the company created a sense of belonging and shared destiny that was a key element to keep everyone working on kaizen even when business events made things too slow or too fast. Although Orry didn't know if it was by coincidence or design, the total amount paid in profit sharing each year was about the same amount of dividends paid to shareholders. He suspected it was by design because the company's founder strongly believed that both human capital and financial capital should share in a company's success.

GROW THE BUSINESS

For external growth, the Wiremold management team had realized that with the communications boom many customers were now installing electrical equipment, cabling, etc. without having to be a licensed electrician because they did not deal with high-voltage installations. Wiremold had been married, so to speak, to the electrical trade and its distribution channels, to which these new customers had no easy access. The strategy was therefore to get closer to customers by connecting to where they purchased. Since building a distribution channel from scratch is costly and difficult – as we know only too well from our own experience – it was easier to acquire existing businesses.

Art's own sensei once told him he had a "good nose for bad businesses." Wiremold was looking for companies without damning quality problems or a damaged image on the market, and, above all, lousy operations based on the dominant batch mentality of the time. They knew that they could cash in on the inventory reduction and the acquisition would pay for itself in a matter of a few years. Consequently, the CEO and his team were very careful about integration, keeping on board as many of the experienced people they could while teaching them another way of working.

Specific answers don't transfer across cultural and industrial contexts – but the way to look for answers does. There is no one technique to change a machine quickly from one production to the next; it all depends on the machine. But SMED as a method can help you discover how to go about it in both cases. When Art bought a company, he would meet every employee personally to reassure them about his "no layoffs" policy and tell them about the profit-sharing plan. Then he would lead a kaizen workshop himself with the company's top management team – and ask them to learn to lead their own. Those who didn't want to could leave. By focusing on teaching a few narrow knowledge points, such as operations flexibility, Wiremold beat the statistics with each successful acquisition.

For new product development to make sense, Orry said, it needs to solve a real customer need with a better solution immediately. Developments for future needs rarely capture the market. For instance, we offered a better way to buy cars, but we didn't suggest not buying cars or making flying cars. He told us about how Wiremold had found a lot of business by reacting quickly to electrical regulatory changes and offering electricians a better (and pricier) solution quicker than its many competitors did. As the sensei says: you don't teach them; you learn from them. You don't educate customers; you learn from them.

In start-up mode, following Eric Ries' lean start-up cycle of build-measure-learn comes quite naturally –

because it's learn or die – even though the measuring piece is often a headache.[27] Build-measure-learn captures the essence of looking for new knowledge points.

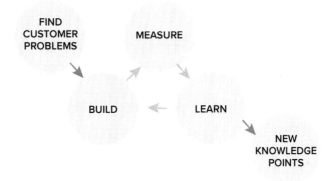

For an established company, the inertia of big development projects makes it tempting to turn this around and ask exactly the wrong question: what other customers could we reach with what we currently know how to do? To stay true to our start-up spirit, we needed to stay focused on relieving *real* customer pain points. What we have learned from our gemba lean efforts is to identify the new knowledge points that will enable us to do so.

---

[27] E. Ries (2011). *The Lean Startup*, Crown Business, New York.

Customer pain points ← Performance → Associates knowledge points

A NEW UNDERSTANDING OF STRATEGY

Orry's approach to strategy is to grow a loyal customer base by being useful to them. Because markets change faster than companies, this is a dynamic strategy. It involves solving day-to-day customer problems to identify what they value and then accelerating how we deliver that value and reduce the cost base through the systematic elimination of waste, both in terms of current products and services and faster development of new products. This can be summarized as CARE:

1. Customer requests come first, then staff's and suppliers', and financial accounting.

2. Accelerate delivery by reducing lead-times.

3. Reduce the total cost base by engaging everyone every day in seeing and eliminating waste.

4. Engineer value by improving the system to make it easy for each person to create more value.

Products, equipment, and systems are the tools through which people deliver value. These need to be engineered carefully so the value flow from frontline staff is unimpeded. Value improves when customers feel they get a good deal for their money: the quality and availability of the service improve while its overall costs diminish. This, indeed, requires a lot of engineering hard work to come up with the right product, made on the right systems with the right tools and methods. But this hard work only occurs if it's guided by the north star of engaging staff in solving customers' problems first and revealing issues by accelerating flows.

"Time is the currency of lean," Orry explains. Looking at lead-times and customer responses and working daily at getting right first-time-to-customers quicker is an approach that simultaneously defines the plan and implements it. There is no separation between strategy and execution. When we shared with him our delivery/discovery model, we agreed we were talking about the same thing. At the planning stage, all we have is a clever idea, but very little solid information, particularly on an innovative venture. The further along you are with execution, the more reality speaks back, and you discover things you had no idea about.

A SWOT strategy is static: you try to make the most of what you already have. CARE is about learning to better solve real customer problems now, which means delivering our base service while being flexible to the customer's singular demands. From this, we can better understand value, which is always mysterious as tastes change with the spirit of the times and technology. This leads to a better understanding of real-life delivery processes and their inflexible points in order to be more responsive to spot demand, both in a wider mix of offering and in how fast we answer. This, in turn, enables us to involve everyone every day in recognizing wasteful activities (for customers and for ourselves) to keep improving the value of what we do: better service at a lower total cost, and remain competitive while making a living. This is a learning strategy.

In early 2019, we realized we had to go beyond improving lead-times and reducing total costs. We needed to think harder about how getting closer to customers could help us clarify what they really valued. The trade-off is between simplicity with a narrow offer (what Google does with a single search bar) versus being a one-stop shop for all customers could want (such as Amazon), which is more convenient for customers but so much harder to manage operationally. Toyota's strategy can be summed up as "one-time customer, lifelong customer," and so they have the widest, least-cannibalized lineup of all automakers (everyone in the family is supposed to find a car they like in the lineup from a Yaris to a Lexus). In digital terms, do you want to be Google, Facebook, Instagram, Apple Pay, etc. – applications that do a single thing? Or the Chinese WeChat, a multipurpose app that includes messaging, social media, and payment: "an app for everything"?

But is either app approach analogous to what we really needed to consider as we scaled up? Could it be less digital and far more personal?

CHAPTER 13:
PERFORMANCE
IS PERSONAL

Many of the top executives we know obsess about performance. They monitor indicators, they track gaps, they demand corrective plans, they snarl and growl when these plans don't work out as expected, and they cut travel allowances and forbid employees to spend time out of the company looking at how other people do things. As the numbers don't improve and they see that their strategy is not bearing fruit, they blame resistance to change and legacy systems. But who can blame them? This is how we were taught to run a business as well.

The real counterintuitive lesson of learning lean on the gemba is that to excel at delivery, you can't only narrowly obsess on delivery as we previously thought. Our customers are people, not machines. Our employees are people, not robots. This obvious fact has three momentous implications:

1. The core part of the product that all customers look for (price, on-time delivery, 100% good products) can be

automated and will benefit from automation, as machines and software respond more consistently to standardized demand.

2. Customers each have singular demands that make the difference between completely satisfied and dissatisfied. These singular demands are how we really help them to solve their problem completely and where we find competitive advantage over alternatives.

3. Employees have the good sense and mental flexibility to respond well to singular situations if they are empowered to do so: encouraged, taught how, and given the tools that allow them to. To stay motivated, people need both a stable routine to their job and some challenging elements requiring creativity, initiative, and doing things their way.

PERFORMANCE RESTS ON WILLINGNESS

People come with positive energy to work, and if the first thing they encounter is their manager's scowl, or the computer doesn't boot up, they start losing that positive energy and end up, at the end of the day, discouraged and disaffected. People also are resilient in so many ways. If the system doesn't allow any space to think, to explore, to express one's creativity, they'll look for it in other ways, such as gaming the system or not showing up for work and so on. In a perverse way, we've discovered that many HR initiatives to improve well-being can be counterproductive, being greeted with cynicism and used to fight the system with the system. The fact of the matter is that people want to be involved in their work – if the company would only let them do so and stop the endless microhumiliations that sap their mood and diminish their energy.

In 2012, we decided to invest and switch to Salesforce, following best practice in the industry. Usual story. At first, it made us move forward visibly, and the staff in the outlets were committed to the change as they had a hand in configuring the early applications. But soon, the system grew unwieldy, people moved on, and we found ourselves in the same situation – again. After early gains, people find the system too rigid and unwieldy to deal with specific customer situations, are often lost in its complexities, and tend to give up on any hope of either mastering it one day or learning to make it work.

There is nothing wrong with Salesforce per se. Just as we now realize, there was nothing wrong with our earlier CRM. The misconception was – and is – focusing exclusively on the system rather than training people – constantly training them to use it and encouraging them to find ways to make it work. People got surprised with unusual situations, misinterpreted what was going on or the impact they could have on the system, and took the wrong action (the right action often being counterintuitive or not encouraged by management). Secondly, connectivity decays daily as decisions are made and changes occur throughout the system without thinking of the impact on interfaces. The only way to correct this is to have people carefully and thoughtfully tend the system all day long and microcorrect ambiguous issues as they appear, continuously.

Digital systems seem magical because you can do wonders with a few lines of code. But they also have fundamental drawbacks we now see:

- *They are complex:* Interactions are everywhere and not always visible.
- *They are dense:* Each system is specialized and very rich in features, yet few people understand or master all features, let alone the underlying code.
- *They are opaque:* No one sees either complexity of interaction or difficulty in the code – contrary to analog

systems, there is no intuitive link between how the system behaves and what drives this behavior.

As a result, business performance easily gets lost in the sheer difficulty of just running the status quo. The hard lesson is to accept that there is no software solution to that kind of scale-up problem. People are the solution. As the sensei often repeats, when people better understand what they do, they work better. To get to better software, we rely on our people to *train* these systems. In ambiguous situations, people can choose to:

• Seek to understand and adapt to what the customer prefers versus following the system blindly.

• Solve issues locally and report obstacles versus work around difficulties and keep their heads down.

• Suggest practical improvement and changes and get involved in making these happen versus accept that "you can't fight the system" and be dissatisfied from one day to the next.

A caricature of this kind of system-centric thinking was our belief in pushing cars to sales outlet as soon as we could. Our enterprise resource planning (ERP) system linked a car with a customer. As soon as the link was established, logistics had to move the car to the outlet – regardless of when the customer expected delivery or the state of the car. We thought that outlets were the best place to deal with customer requests and fix problems on cars when and if needed. This wrong-headed misconception left the sales-point manager completely overburdened with full parking lots, repairs they didn't know how to complete, annoyed customers, and so on. We felt that the system worked and that people were not smart enough in dealing with the last mile of satisfying customers. The system was scalable – people were not.

Yes, we need systems upgrades, no debate. But first and foremost, we learned we need people's willingness to work with the new tool – to adopt it. Willingness is an asset that we need to apply to any structural change for it to pay off as intended. As leaders, willingness is *our job.* As we refined our thinking on trust, we narrowed willingness to two basic dimensions: people's trust in their own self-reliance (I'm confident you'll get there, keep looking) and in their leader's commitment (we're not going to let this go and look for easier gains; we really need to crack this).

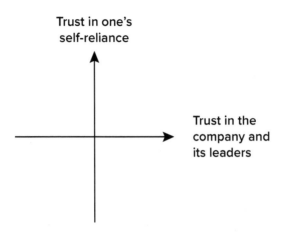

Changing our own attitude about willingness has had an impact. We accepted that a growth culture rests on the belief that 1) learning is a worthwhile use of our time, and 2) learning will happen if we keep trying, which, in itself, completely changes the learning process. As we changed, so did our management team and our employee satisfaction results.

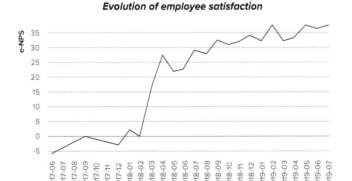

Evolution of employee satisfaction

Our score for employee satisfaction (the e-NPS) is calculated by asking people, "How likely would you recommend AramisAuto as a pleasant company to work for?" We calculate the percentage of "ambassadors," employees that have answered 9 or 10; the percentage of nonambassadors, answering from 0 to 6; and subtract the latter percentage from the former.

As we are a visible company, our work method intrigued a journalist, who gathered comments from our staff. "There hasn't been much internal communication on any change of management method," said Antoine, a commercial manager, "but I've noticed that when top management visits my branch, the discussion has shifted from reviewing results to discussing obstacles to achieve results and a clear intention to better understand our problems." Antoine remembers former times when instructions were given top-down without a good understanding of what that entailed. "Our associates realized we cared about what they thought, and we got fast buy in." Clémence, who joined the company two years ago, was surprised by our "welcome problems" attitude, so different with what she had experienced elsewhere. The examples they chose to share with the journalist reflect the level of detail we're trying to work at. One recounts making a mistake in one of her first jobs for the company but being greeted with a supportive smile from Brigitte, the head of HR, who then patiently explained how to get it right. The other recounts how there was a delivery failure on certain cars, but as the branch team analyzed the problem they discovered that a new software patch had been wrongly configured and so shipping documents were automatically set aside by the system. No drama.[28]

For leaders, it is hard to imagine that real-life performance is forged at this level of detail: creating a safe space for people to make mistakes and learn, delving into problems to figure out their cause, and improving. Also, the fact that taking an interest in such problems makes us see the business differently and leads to strategic insights is equally hard to fathom unless you've experienced it. Contrary to what we thought, lean is not a better delivery system: it's an education system that teaches people how to find the knowledge points that will ensure better delivery.

[28] L. Zohin (March 6, 2019). "AramisAuto mise sur le comment plutôt que sur les résultats," *Entreprises et Carrières.*

LEAN IS AN EDUCATION SYSTEM

Kids learn from what they're told – they're taught to recognize concepts that are not immediately intuitive, such as the fact that the moon that you see is really a small, natural satellite hanging unsupported in space and rotating around the world. Adults, however, learn very differently because their minds no longer are a blank slate. Adults are steeped in experience, and they have prior knowledge of almost everything.

To get adults to learn, you've got to structure work as postgraduate education: give each person a difficult problem to crack, a study case, which they work on as part of their normal job. This is what A3s are really for: as a personal learning project.

The Toyota Production System (TPS) is a starting point to find typical problems in our business – problems that will occur at anytime, anywhere, to anyone, such as giving customers a better welcome or sourcing popular cars more effectively. Toyota's own production system, as it's taught by its sensei, clarifies these problems into:

• Improve customer loyalty through complete satisfaction by safety, quality, cost, and lead-time improvements.

- Improve capital productivity by reducing lead-time with just-in-time techniques.
- Improve labor productivity by building in quality with jidoka techniques.
- Improve employee engagement by voluntary contribution to quality and total cost reduction with kaizen and standards.
- Improve teamwork across the hierarchy and functions by greater mutual trust from 5S, problem-solving, and enablers.

These typical problems are *troublesome* problems: problems that will never have an easy solution. They create an architecture for problem-based learning because they are an endless trove of learning challenges, which then break down into very specific technical problems – which people can take on board one at a time in order to learn.

Lean is essentially a learning system devised by Toyota to encourage kaizen: voluntary participation of all employees in improving quality and reducing costs. It's a system because the various aspects correlate to each other, and you can't quite progress without understanding the connections. The system frames the what, how, and why so that each person can contribute a creative idea to improving their work processes:

1. Satisfy customers completely: The goal of all our efforts is the total satisfaction of customers by offering both innovative products and services and excellent delivery in terms of safety, quality, delivery, cost, energy efficiency, and connectivity.

Exploring value for
CUSTOMER SATISFACTION

2. By visualizing just-in-time and built-in quality: Just-in-time aims to reduce lead-time by pulling and visualizing schedules so that people can see problems and get closer to single-piece flow. Built-in quality is achieved through the andon system of calling out attention on every issue and turning the management line into a chain of help to train and problem-solve.

Exploring value for
CUSTOMER SATISFACTION

Visualizing processes and reducing lead-time by **JUST-IN-TIME**

Right first time and visualizing problems by **BUILT-IN QUALITY**

3. In order to prompt employees to propose creative ideas: This is promoted by leveling their workload (so they don't suffer from a boom-and-bust schedule) and both training them to known standards and involving them in team kaizen activities.

Exploring value for
CUSTOMER SATISFACTION

Visualizing processes and reducing lead-time by
JUST-IN-TIME

Right first time and visualizing problems by
BUILT-IN QUALITY

Employee satisfaction by engagement/involvement:
LEVELING, STANDARDS, AND KAIZEN

4. Which rests on constant efforts to grow mutual trust: This type of relationship between management and associates comes about by encouraging associates to improve their own workspaces through 5S, creating space to think for kaizen, and supporting them with enabling processes so they can do their job well without having to fight the system.

Exploring value for
CUSTOMER SATISFACTION

Visualizing processes and reducing lead-time by JUST-IN-TIME

Right first time and visualizing problems by BUILT-IN QUALITY

Employee satisfaction by engagement/involvement: LEVELING, STANDARDS, AND KAIZEN

Growing mutual trust: 5S, PROBLEM-SOLVING, ENABLERS

As in any discipline, the basic blocks of what, how, and why have to be learned to fully master the lean frame through which to look at our processes. We can't say it's been easy, and we've stopped counting the hours we've spent with the sensei working through each step of the system, the interactions between the elements, and then working out what that means on the shop floor. We need to learn the techniques to answer:

1. How to understand value more deeply and come up with responses?

2. How to build in quality in a product or service?

3. How to pull value rather than push activities?

4. How to engage and involve employees in their work?

5. How to build on a foundation of mutual trust?

For instance, although we've been successful with pulling cars through our logistics process, we are still learning the intricacies of kanban in the plant and discovering new, more detailed questions where everyone is stumped. But the teams don't shy away from the challenge; they try and think, try and think, and come up with surprising answers – it's ongoing, and making sure it doesn't stop and backslide is our job. As the sensei says, it's not just an intellectual question, but one of emotional motivation: how do we keep the teams wanting to continue to progress? Part of the answer is us better understanding the system, what it does, and how it's supposed to work to give them a clearer sense of direction: what are we after and where to look for answers.

We have all been taught about the power of intrinsic motivation (motivated to do something for its own sake or because we find it personally rewarding) over extrinsic motivation (doing things to either avoid punishment or to earn a reward). In recent years, empirical theory of motivation has evolved and has become more specific. Most people seek to satisfy innate needs for:

- *Competence:* Control their environment to achieve outcomes and seek mastery.
- *Relatedness:* Connect, interact, and care (and be cared for) with people around us.
- *Autonomy:* Be in control of our own lives and act in harmony with our fullest selves.

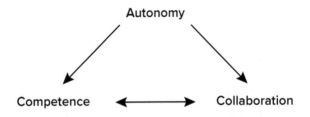

The explicit, ultimate aim of this system is to *motivate* employees to learn and develop themselves to the fullest of their abilities.

A DIFFERENT THINKING PROCESS

When we started the business, our livelihood depended on every extra car sold, so, yes, we were naturally focused on keeping every customer happy. For a short while, the issue > decide > solution chain was very short because we worked directly with customers, found and purchased the cars ourselves, and even sometimes did the delivery. When we started organizing purchasing and transportation, reaction remained very quick. And, as we developed the digital side, here again "test and learn" was the name of the game. When we launched a new marketing claim or a new advertising campaign, we'd know really quick if it was working or not – fail fast, indeed. It was fun. It was scary. It was exhilarating. We stumbled in every ditch, and we had a ball.

What we completely missed when we started hiring other people was that our own learning did not translate. We told them what to do and what our practices were (embarrassingly, we've kept our folders of "standards" at the office). But we never realized that without the experience of mistakes and pitfalls we'd had before coming up with this or that way of doing things, the "best practice" taught them very little. Indeed, we often got very frustrated with their lack of common sense in how they interpreted and applied the standards, which led us inevitably to tighter control – then more command and more control.

We had no way of knowing that learning occurs from making mistakes and solving problems, not applying known solutions. The known practice is a good starting point, but chances are the problem you're facing is unique and will need some insight and initiative to have a good outcome, not just an OK output. As you can see in any Hollywood flick, the leader is the guy who defines the situation (here's how it is), makes a decision (here's what we're going to do), drives it through to completion (make it so or else), and then when things don't work out and complications arise, deals with whatever comes (and does the fancy footwork). At the movies, the complications are what makes it fun – watching the hero somehow turn disaster into success from sheer guts and luck. But movies have that magic ingredient – a screenwriter. In real life, complications add up and multiply, and things more often go from bad to worse than magically from worse to better.

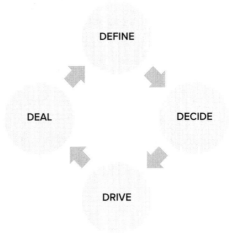

The process starts in the heads of visionary leaders as they define situations in their terms for everyone else and firmly come to decisions. Then this decision must move from theory to real world through execution, where it encounters reality, and everything fights back. For instance, we thought it was time to change our ERP – everyone was complaining about how slow it was, with as much as five seconds to load certain pages and so on. We had *defined* the problem as "ERP = legacy system, so we need to upgrade to a state-of-the art system." We then asked a consultant to define the specs for the new system and looked at how we would finance the (huge) bill for the transition. We had to *decide* to go forward or not.

In the end, we didn't do it. But we can imagine how the rest of the story goes. The literature is full of ERP projects that go disastrously wrong, both in terms of stopping operations in their tracks and awful over-costs. Researchers looked into 1,471 such projects and, alarmingly, found that one in six was a "black swan" – a project turned catastrophically bad, such as Levi Strauss' $5 million upgrade that turned into a $200 million loss when it had to integrate with Walmart's own systems.[29] One in six – a scary number. Senior management drives forcefully the implementation, as it runs into unexpected issues and reality fights back – and then they *deal* with the consequences: fancy footwork and blame allocation.

From learning the TPS with our sensei's help, we had the "Aha!" realization that everyone in the company needed their own learning curve. As leaders, we needed to create the conditions for learning, not just dish out answers. This means learning a completely different thought process that starts with reality by finding problems, such as mis-delivery because of a wrongly configured new software patch. From discussing these problems with the ground teams, we learn to see the elephants in the room, and we face them. We then frame them in a way that everyone understands what the problem is and the direction of the solution we're looking for. And so we can form a solution from everyone's local countermeasures and craft a new way of doing the work as we discover and share new knowledge points. We start the thinking cycle with reality and end with reality.

[29] B. Flyvberg & A. Budzier (September 2011).
"Why Your IT Project May Be Riskier than You Think," *Harvard Business Review.*
https://hbr.org/2011/09/why-your-it-project-may-be-riskier-than-you-think

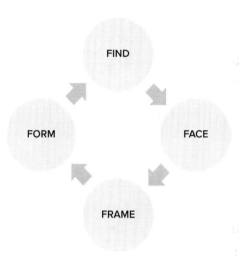

While this is nothing more than empirical scientific thinking, in the business world it lacks the stylishness of decisiveness everyone seems to expect. On the other hand, this is an inclusive method that involves all associates in both defining the problems and looking for solutions. Whenever we discover a new problem at the workplace, we cannot help jumping to a solution – this is how the mind works. The real effort is in keeping mum, saying "tell me more," and finding other people's answers more interesting than your own – the key moment that radically changes every conversation.

With the ERP upgrade, Jean-Michel, the IT director, started by finding the issues. He looked into the most problematic cases with users one problem at a time.

He then *faced* the issues pertaining to the system, as opposed to blaming the users for not using it well. He *framed* it in terms of looking at the user interface and retro-engineering how the screen came up: what needed to be calculated for every screen and what did not. Having grasped the generic problem, he involved his teams in looking at each interface, simplifying the process that brought the screens to users, and testing with users which solutions they preferred. In the end, they achieved a 50% improvement in productivity of treatment of orders and an 80% performance improvement of the system – without upgrade. The key point is that IT teams had to learn a lot more than they knew about how the system really worked and what could be done to make it perform better, case by case.

THE SYSTEM IS A STARTING POINT, NOT AN END POINT

The lean tools are a starting point, not an end in themselves. When we first met the sensei, he asked whether we wanted to win or whether we were happy just to stay in the game. We wanted to win. Then he asked us whether we were ready to change – as opposed to promoting alibi activities in order not to change. We told him we were ready to change but we didn't know what. He had no answer to that, other than we needed to find it out.

Years down the line, we know a bit better. We've had to learn to practice the lean system to change our attitude to problems. They were not there for us to solve, but for *everyone*. Our job was to create the conditions for a growth culture of problem solvers.

Ask yourself: How many people do you manage? Are you running things with just the few brains around you and an army of hands?

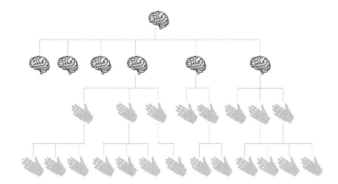

Or are you engaging every brain in growing your business – to make it sustainable and profitable?

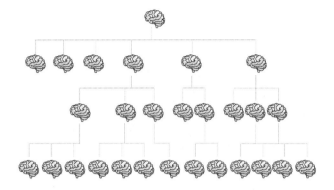

A lean system creates the conditions to engage every brain by orienting towards customer value; by visualizing problems and engaging people in solving them; and by creating safe spaces to work, think, and create to involve people with their teams.

Decisiveness often hides fixation on early diagnostics that are almost always wrong. The only things solid and unmoving in life are our ideas – reality itself is endlessly changing and surprising. It's not what you don't know that gets you into real trouble – it's what you think is true that just isn't so.

The real scale-up challenge for us was to learn to learn – how to engage everyone in the company in learning and then learning collectively to perform as a unit. But for this to happen, we had to stop thinking in people's stead and not solve every problem in our minds, on our own. The real point of kaizen, we've now learned, is not the immediate improvement of a detailed problem. It is to start engaging the teams first and then connecting people with ideas to support their coming together in forming smart solutions. It's the discovery of the knowledge points that will enable us to solve all such problems consistently and move on to the next issue.

Change your mind: you can't learn in other people's stead – they have to follow their own learning journey. And, yes, supporting them in doing so is taking *decisive* – and radical – action. The secret of a successful scale-up is to learn to scale up *learning.*

CHAPTER 14:
SHARE INNOVATION

Home delivery was our worst good idea to date. Back in 2015, when we were struggling on all fronts, we reacted as many CEOs do – we dreamed up a new feature, thinking it would save us. Home delivery came up frequently in our conversations with friends and business partners. Our overarching goal was to disrupt and transform car purchasing, and, well, e-commerce websites all delivered – so why didn't we? Looking back, we must admit that none of our customers ever asked for it, other than a few well-off acquaintances who didn't feel like leaving the city center, where they lived, to find one of our sales points in the burbs.

Our wishful thinking about home delivery also was driven by the high cost and effort of opening new sales points, and we felt that covering our entire territory would take forever. We wanted to grow faster than that. In typical define-and-decide fashion, we decided we had to offer home delivery to fully exploit the potential of our territory. With hindsight, this was traditional strategy at its plainest.

On paper, it made perfect sense. It would also pressure our competitors and give the marketing department something to talk about – remember that at the time we were sustaining our growth mainly through communication spend.

Eric Ries' *The Lean Startup*[30] made a big splash in the digital world when it came out in 2011, and we were enthused by its ideas. Indeed, one of us lobbied hard to get it translated quickly and wrote the preface to the French edition. To reduce risk-taking and learn from customers, the book recommends testing leap-of-faith assumptions by building a minimum viable product (MVP). This is a bare-bones functional product that runs the full cycle of build-measure-learn with minimum effort and quick development time, which generates proof of concept in terms of both the value-to-customers hypothesis and the growth hypothesis. Our proof-of-concept set-up was very positive, and, in a boardroom meeting, the executive committee signed up for a launch of the new home delivery service in March 2016, with the expectation that it would strongly contribute to a 30% sales growth expected within a year.

[30] E. Ries (2011). *The Lean Startup,* Crown Business, New York.

As we were working with lean consultants at the time, we also saw the launch as an opportunity to accelerate our new product development, and we gave the project team three months to launch the service. A VP was named to follow the project closely. After *defining* and *deciding*, we would do what was needed to *drive* the project.

We thought we had applied lean start-up principles, but we had missed the most important lean idea: *get out of the building* – in lean terms, go and see the real thing in the real place with real people. Home delivery is actually a very complex process. It cumulates our own logistics process, which at the time was totally out of control, and the customer's own logistics. We were struggling to deliver cars to 23 sales points, and our main customer complaint was how long it took. With home delivery, we added thousands of potential new delivery points at once. In order to scale, we delegated the delivery logistics to a contractor who simply couldn't cope: lead-time at our sales points doubled, the contractor's poor service attitude drove customers crazy, and customer satisfaction plummeted rapidly.

And we learned the hard way from all of this that ... few customers actually asked for home delivery. We discovered that they actually liked taking ownership of their car in our offices, which was a safe place to make the transaction, deal with the paperwork with someone, and get reassurance that this person will take care of the inevitable problems. Word got around quickly that the few customers who tried home delivery were very unhappy with it, so our commercial staff quickly did what they could to avoid offering the service and advised their customers to pick up their car at a point of sales.

We should have pulled the plug, but by now some of our competitors were offering home delivery as well, so we let the business barely get by, used by less than 10% of our customers along with a lousy satisfaction index.

Then at the turn of 2019, Juliette, the lean officer who had supported the teams in their pull flow implementations, got frustrated with her lack of progress with the last bit of the chain – home delivery. Although quite junior, she'd done a fantastic job in getting the sales points to adopt visual management and work more closely with logistics at headquarters, and she felt she wanted to try hands-on management as opposed to a staff role. A quiet, cheerful executive with a forceful personality and whose good nature and persistence usually wore down the opposition, Juliette seemed like a good shot to fix a business we still believed in: if it could be done properly, home delivery would definitely add value to our customers and move us forward in our vision to completely transform the car-purchasing experience.

We knew this would be quite a stretch and a steep learning curve. Juliette would have to learn what it means to manage a team – a thoroughly demotivated and negative team at that – at the same time as she would have to tackle the logistics of home delivery. And to tell the truth, she did struggle. Fresh from her experience with setting the pull flow of cars in the sales points, she was taken aback by the team's initial lack of interest and cooperation. Eventually, she took a step back and listened to her VPs' advice: fix the team first.

As she had learned from working with us and the sensei on the logistics flow, she looked at this challenge from her team's point of view. She framed the question in terms of "what makes you want to come to work in the morning?" She came up with four reasons:

1. It's a nice place with a good work atmosphere, and I am happy to join people I like or respect.

2. The team's mission is clear (and I know it).

3. At the end of the day, I can tell whether it was a successful day or not.

4. My manager clears roadblocks I don't know how to handle and helps me make progress.

Having outlined the team's frame, she looked at each person in turn and thought about what she had to change in her own behavior as a team leader to make people feel things were progressing on these four dimensions. She realized she had been making many inadvertent faux pas in how she first handled the team, assuming they would naturally accept her authority and the solutions she brought from her previous experience in logistics. For instance, she was fully backed by her hierarchy, all the way to the CEO, but had not expected this would make the team more resentful, not less. The team had been poorly managed and demotivated for too long and was resentful of everything, until she finally accepted that the solutions she was bringing over from her sales-point work simply would not be accepted and, actually, might not work there.

Juliette went back to square one and focused on problem-finding. The long and short of it was that a home delivery, for which we charged $50, took a fortnight longer than picking the car up at a sales point. To add insult to injury, the delivery itself rarely went right, with missing manuals, for instance, or unpleasant drivers. She worked with the team to find easy wins. For instance, they could accelerate the first phone call to schedule the delivery and have more time to organize the logistics. We also had made good progress in our logistics, and she knew the logistics team leaders well, so they started working out specific solutions for home delivery. On the team front, she got them to buy in to a routine of 5S and owning their working space, which started to make the team come together. Fortunately, the most negative person left, and the internal dynamic of the team changed.

With a better understanding of the situation, Juliette faced the elephant in the room – the relationship with our external partner. It had become purely transactional, triggering low-road mechanisms of defensiveness and passive-aggressiveness in which each side saw themselves as victims being persecuted by the other. Our side felt that they paid them well enough; surely, they could do the job. The other side felt no one understood or cared about their very real everyday troubles. To counter that, Juliette started a program of mutual gemba visits and a list of singular problems to solve together as well as on-the-job training. In a classic case of reframing, problem-solving after problem-solving, she succeeded at turning "vendor=contractor" into "vendor=partner."

Juliette's team results speak for themselves: deliveries doubled, on-time delivery rose from 40% to above 70%, and the Net Promoter Score (NPS) doubled as well.

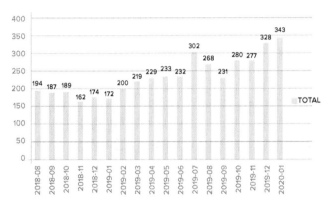

Evolution of monthly home deliveries

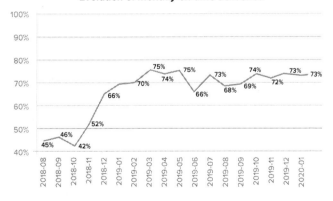

Evolution of monthly on-time deliveries

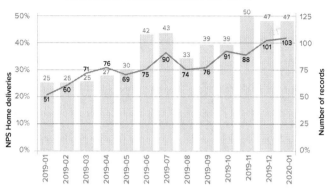

Evolution of customer satisfaction (NPS)

Home-delivery measurements aren't quite yet matching that of sales, but they'll get there. They're also expanding the range of the services they offer to customers to continue to facilitate purchase, such as maintenance contracts, special packs, and so on. The key lesson for the team is that they, quite logically, believed that having more steps in the process, they would never be able to do as well as the branches. We don't hear this any longer as, knowledge point by knowledge point, the team is learning to better control its flow and is already performing better than our most backwards sales points.

INNOVATION IS NOT VALUE UNTIL IT WORKS FOR CUSTOMERS

The deeper learning for us about innovation is that an innovative idea or a new use of technology is not an innovation until it's turned into concrete value for customers. This creates an interesting dilemma. One thing we know well in tech is that we can't ask customers what they want, because they actually don't know. As Henry Ford once quipped, if he'd asked his customers what they wanted they would have asked for a faster horse. Successful new products or services usually stem from a wider reframe. Bill Gates dreamed of a PC on every desk. Steve Jobs wanted to get rid of the interface barrier between humans and computers. Page and Brin wanted to mine the web for relevance. Bezos wants to create the ultimate everything store, and so on. These frames are powerful. They lead you to pursue some ideas and ignore some others. Our frame of "purchase your car on the internet" led us to think of home delivery as with any other e-commerce company.

"What" comes from a sense of "where" we want to go. But the "how" depends on customers, employees, and partners. If we don't develop these broad ideas by solving real problems for customers right *NOW!* the innovation might be clever but will not be adopted.

Amazon's Fire phone. Facebook's phone. Apple's Newton. Google+, Google Glass. Microsoft's Zune – the list is endless. The technology is there, and people are out there looking for the next sweet spot.

TECH-DRIVEN
VISION

VALUE FOR
COSTUMERS

As you scale up, every functional department wants to be innovative. As a result, you tend to generate many projects with tenuous links with value to customers. We regularly uncover some in our A3 presentations. For instance, we thought we could better exploit our CRM with a customer sponsorship program to encourage them to recommend us to their friends and relatives which, in the end, confused customers more than anything else and turned out to be very costly. On the other hand, you want to keep generating ideas and trying stuff out.

To succeed, innovation needs to pass four hurdles:

1. Technological breakthrough: Turn new tech into a useful service.

2. *Internal acceptance:* Staff see the potential of the innovation and integrate it within their own systems and help to deliver it to customers.

3. *Customer adoption:* Customers will test and progressively adopt the new feature as they find a way to use it and value the job it does for them.

4. *Market embrace:* A tipping-point number of customers now expect this new feature as a new normal, and all competitors must bundle it in their offer.

We started the business gathering emails and phoning customers back. Our big break came when we learned to work with SEA (search engine advertising), just at a time when Google's solution became dominant on the web and exploded overnight. Simultaneously, we had to learn to master car purchasing (Where are the cars, and how do we live off the price at which they're offered?) and logistics (How do we move a car across the country quickly and efficiently?). A service is, in fact, a blend of features, driven by tech.

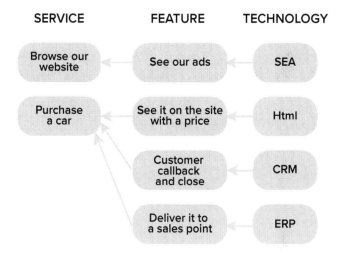

SERVICE	FEATURE	TECHNOLOGY
Browse our website	See our ads	SEA
Purchase a car	See it on the site with a price	Html
	Customer callback and close	CRM
	Deliver it to a sales point	ERP

As systems are increasingly needed to do every new thing, innovation becomes increasingly hard work because, as Juliette found out, the new features need to integrate with existing systems in ways customers find useful. This requires internal support – in this instance, making the changes in Salesforce to visualize the kanban.

Technology is evolving fast, and as it does, some things that were simply too costly to do quickly before become affordable, such as having top-quality photos of cars displayed on our site. For the past couple of years, we've been experimenting with data tech to improve our pricing.

On cars, for instance, we now have detailed knowledge of car prices and sales lead-times. We can capture spot car prices every day on the web, and so build a model of market price and identify best buys in a category. We can also track browsing patterns and look at how often a car appears in searches, how many clicks, how often it is looked at, and so on. Data allows us to reduce considerably the incertitude of the car's sales price as a function of how long we expect to keep it on the site. Just a few years back, this curve was simply impossible to calculate – neither the data nor the processing power were available. This allows us to better price the car upfront and then quickly update its price as the context changes.

Making the data tech for this feature work hinges, here again, on discovering specific knowledge points. Firstly, contrary to what we thought, price isn't the only important variable. The competitive environment of any given car on the website matters just as much: i.e., if a car has no competing model, it will go for a higher price. We learned to add our own offer to the price information from the market to calculate the price at any given time – and to adjust it as cars come and go on the page.

Also contrary to what we believed, the unusual features of a car, such as outlandish colors, don't necessarily drive the price down – in certain cases, they can actually increase the car's value. For example, a red car is usually priced lower than a grey one on the assumption that it doesn't sell as well; but it could well sell for more because of its rarity value – it doesn't appear as often on the market. Depending on the car models, this is true not only for color but other features and options as well.

The data tech has real potential to radically improve how we both buy and sell cars by improving our pricing know-how – thus, we believe, giving us a significant advantage over our competitors. However, just as with home delivery, cracking the technical problem is only the first step. We now need to convince the rest of the company to adopt the feature and use it routinely. This is far from obvious, as the new tech doesn't interface seamlessly with the current work habits of purchasing or the systems that display cars on the site.

An interesting observation from one of Juliette's team veterans who'd been there since the start of home delivery is that the project, in order to succeed, had been treated as an internal start-up, and so developed its own procedures and systems. This is not necessarily a bad thing, but what we did learn is that home delivery's success was dependent on our own logistics capability. Juliette made it work because 1) she had been part of the logistics improvement effort, 2) so she knew she could make it work by 3) benefitting from logistics progress, and 4) from the relationships she had formed across the company by participating in our "fix logistics" effort.

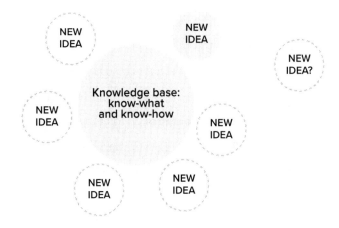

Learning remains very proximal. Every new idea requires the rest of our capabilities to thrive. As Orry told us, successfully growing the business, whether with new products or external acquisitions, heavily depends on how well you improve your base. Many CEOs think that in order to escape poor performance in a "red ocean" (where all the sharks tear bloodily at each other), they can leap into a "blue ocean" of easy picking and no competitors by a feat of technical prowess. We now know you can't. Your ability to turn innovative ventures into value largely depends on how good you are at what you do right now.

IT'S NOT HOW MUCH YOU KNOW, BUT HOW WELL YOU LEARN

The other wider lesson from Juliette's experience that we are seeing more broadly now is that knowledge doesn't transfer. Knowledge points, the basis of our performance, are local. They don't apply well across domains. What does transfer is 1) the belief they exist, and so the growth mindset to go looking for them, and 2) the learning method. When the team leader let go of trying to apply the knowledge points she'd picked up at the sales points and started reproducing her learning curve – not her knowledge – the situation opened up, and the Chinese finger trap loosened itself.

If we're serious about succeeding, we always need to remind ourselves to go back to singular problem-solving, one by one, to find the problems; discover the real difficulty and face it; frame it for others to understand what we're trying to do and what we're after; and form solutions from their initiatives. In doing this repeatedly, our ability to solve problems and distinguish real countermeasures from problem workarounds accelerates. Lean tools – such as 5S, kanban, and andon – are essential for this acceleration to occur and create a visual environment to reveal problems so that people can take them up.

In hindsight, some of these changes seem obvious to us now and have been articulated by many before us (the problem-solving process), but other aspects had to be experienced by our teams in the trenches before they truly could be witnessed and understood (the transfer of how to learn rather than the knowledge that learning creates). Our ability to take on and eventually grasp the latter type of changes is what has supported our upward evolution.

CHAPTER 15:
WHAT WE KNOW NOW

Our early innovation model was straightforward: intuition **>** execution. It started from the inspiration to do something, then hitting upon the right technical intuition and driving it through the company until it worked – to some extent. This is the classic genius-driven model of innovation.

While it might work in start-up mode, as the company grows this model simply becomes untenable. Systems become too well established, politics are unavoidable, and customers expect continuity of service – disrupting existing services for the sake of introducing new features is simply unacceptable. Practicing lean taught us to radically change our understanding of innovation: we need ideas from all our staff, every day.

A SUGGESTIONS-BASED INNOVATION MODEL

This new vision of innovation – suggestion-based innovation – starts on the gemba, at the workplace. One of the key innovations of our site was the quality of the car photos we present to browsers. We knew all along that photos were an important part of our value proposition – we could see how our sales teams used the photos on the site to look for the right car for each customer. One day, we were chatting about it with one of the founders of the largest e-commerce site in town, and he said, "Online, we sell photos, not products." This throwaway line struck us deeply, and we took that as a challenge: Did we really sell photos online? Or did we assume we sold cars, and photos were just the first step on the sales ladder?

Before online car photo

After online car photo

When we started looking into it, we realized that not only the quality of photos on the site was often disappointing, but it also took three full days to get them up online. We set ourselves the task to improve the customer's online experience with a step change in photo quality, as well as to reduce the lead-time from three days to 30 minutes, which meant raising the bar quite dramatically.

To visualize the problem, we cleared a room, set up a specific obeya, and established a quality target (360° photos and high-resolution photos of issues on cars) and a process target (short work content and short lead-time to get them on site). We then mapped the value stream to visualize every step in the process and the issues related to that step. The refurbishment site took the lead, but we established a fortnightly tempo of visits and reviews from the headquarters teams as well.

Fred, the project leader on site, encountered endless problems. He would post the new procedure on the wall in the photo studio only to discover new issues, including insufficient lighting, dirt in the room, awkward shooting positions, hard-to-capture defects, and unwieldy equipment (such as a rotating table that needed the operator to hold his finger on the button while the thing turned ever so slowly).

With hindsight, everything seems easy, but as you experience it, every obstacle seems impossible to pass. The rotating table's engine doesn't have enough power – what can be done? LED lighting is too low – what can be done? Uploading time of high-resolution photos is too long – what can be done? As leaders, we had no idea of how to solve any of these technical issues, but we realized that if we kept coming back and reinforcing that the original objectives were critical to the business, people would nod, scratch their head, and get back to it. We experienced firsthand what it means to align personal fulfillment and company success.

And problems did get cracked as Fred and Rémi, the plant manager, tackled the mechanical issues, such as finding a clever way to better use the table rotor, and the photographers themselves came up with a steady stream of good ideas that were tested, considered, and either adopted or improved on. They changed how the lab worked, rewired it entirely, changed the access control. They included all photo studio equipment in the plant's maintenance plan, solving many equipment-failure issues and lead-time obstacles. They installed a photovoltaic inverter. They fitted in a large screen in the shooting zone to see results live.

But we also discovered that supporting the local team in solving all these problems was not enough – we also had an adoption problem, both by the operators who initially saw an increased work content while the issues were being fixed and the headquarters' website teams that struggled with new interfaces to take full benefit of the new photos. Typically, people would take early issues with a new attempt as a sure sign of failure – and on occasion would argue that it was impossible. Then, because of the fast-learning process, Fred would iterate quickly and change the operating standard – which would make the rest of the people involved, from web designers to suppliers, grumble about the "instability of our process" and take it as an excuse to wait for us to make up our mind to fix the bugs on their end. Understandable reactions, all of them, and, to be fair, we realized that we behaved the same way with some other attempts at innovation in the company. This made us realize that, after making it work, a serious hurdle is to get the rest of the company to adopt the innovation – long before it even reaches customers.

At some point in this messy moving-forward-and-solving-obstacles-one-by-one process, Rémi, the plant manager, and Guillaume, our website guru, realized that the price of 360° Wi-Fi cameras had dropped steeply – they convinced us this was the tech that we needed to achieve our lead-time objectives, and, indeed, it worked. Interestingly, as we now look back and compare successful versus unsuccessful innovation attempts, we see the latter tend to put the tech first – a solution looking for a problem. In successes, the tech disruption often arrives late, when the fundamental problem is well understood. We tend to forget it now, but the entire company was first premised on phone selling – the internet solutions that made us who we are today emerged when Google cracked the SEA problem.

In hindsight, we can discern a specific model for innovation in fast-changing environments:

1. Raise the bar: From gemba walk to gemba walk, keep raising the bar. As a Toyota executive once told us, 99.5% delivery success rate is 5,000 fails per million. Don't pressure people or be a jerk about it, but raise the bar and, equally important, be vigilant against accidentally lowering the bar for tactical reasons. Customers are hooked on value – keep giving them more.

2. Visualize processes and visit frequently: To make step one – raise the bar – a reality, you have to go there and get people to visualize the process (every key process, everywhere); clarify your control points (physical control points as opposed to reporting reviews, as we did with parking spots); and look into issues. People will tell you what needs to be fixed (they'll typically phrase it as "We need to apply my favored solution"), which you learn to ignore and dive deeper into the "Why?" and "How?" of the issue.

3. Repeatedly explain the challenge: Because they are swamped with instructions, injunctions, and contradictory demands, people give up easily, particularly when they don't feel particularly self-confident. Repeating endlessly that a specific challenge is a matter of life or death for the company is essential to maintaining the sense of urgency and importance without which efforts simply disappear in the messiness of everyday work.

4. Encourage suggestions: Good ideas seldom come all pretty and dressed for the prom. Typically, new ideas sound silly, irrelevant, or unscalable. It is key to continue to encourage suggestions and to support new insights and initiatives because you never know where the final solution will come from (if you did, you'd already know these solutions). People are timid with their suggestions – this is perfectly normal and to be expected. It takes strong managerial attitudes of curiosity and being intrigued as well as a little encouragement to get them to actually try the new stuff we so desperately need for innovation.

Suggestion presentation during a gemba walk

5. Support adoption by the organization: A critical step we were never taught in any of our management courses, books, or conferences was how carefully internal adoption needs to be managed. The traditional assumption is that you can force technical innovation down the throat of your employees: here's the new system – use it. Failure to get the company to full-heartedly adopt an innovation and adapt all other systems to it most likely will result in market failure as well. As a start-up, we never had this problem, because we did everything ourselves or with a small team. As a scale-up, this has become a huge problem, and one that we work on daily with the obeya meeting room.

6. Be on the lookout for the technical insight: Most a priori tech solutions, we've found, are clever but plain wrong. To work, the solution has to fit a certain context, which means that out of all the options touted by vendors, only a small number will fit the bill. Don't force it. Connect the dots and wait for a technical insight – it will come, though not necessarily where or from whom you expect it. Google's "These ads suck" is an essential part of innovation management. The problem comes first, and then you recognize the insight.

7. Pass on the value to the customers: Don't be tempted to keep the value for yourself. Pass the value on. For your innovation to succeed, customers must adopt it, then the market must adopt it as an "of course" to the point that your competitors are forced to do the same. The only way to control the future is to create it, so when something works better, immediately look for ways more value can be released to customers.

THE ATTITUDE OF THE LEADERS
MAKES THE DIFFERENCE

Innovation is a key challenge in today's society – at the rate we're overconsuming resources, we'd better continue to be very innovative and commit to a circular economy if we want to maintain our current lifestyles – switch away from emission-producing energies, throw less (much less) plastic in the oceans, find new ways to fight antibiotic-resistant infections; the list is long. And yet, no one seems to have found a clear path to systematic innovation so far. The literature oscillates between three poles: the visionary dictatorial genius, the controlled gated process, and the "20% time for employees to try whatever they want" approach.

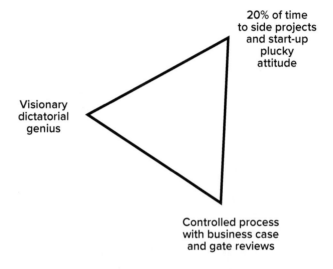

We believe that lean's challenge-and-support offers a viable alternative to scale innovation. Looking at innovation from the adoption view, we can see where to focus our efforts:

Technology insights	New technologies are adopted by engineers when engineers see a clear opportunity to turn a cost (or ease) advantage into a new feature to get a job done more easily or to do routinely something that couldn't be done before.
Value analysis	New features need to be adopted by others in the company to fully integrate with existing systems and tools as a whole. Fixing problems in technologies now currently used in production teaches us how to adopt new features faster.
Value engineering	Work with key customers to look for new ways to deliver value, to help them adopt innovative ideas, and to understand what they really find useful (as opposed to what they say they'd like) to make the new feature an obvious staple of our service.
Marketing investment	Market our successes with customers widely until the market accepts the new feature as a given and demands it from all competing offers.

This dynamic, lean view of innovation helps us to understand where we need to focus in order to create the conditions for innovation. Being innovative is more than being creative with technology and inventive with features. It also requires being people- and social-smart to turn engineering technical insights into actual value for customers, and the efforts of everyone in the company to integrate the innovation in our existing systems.

CONTINUOUS INNOVATION

When we started working with the sensei, one of our first insights was that pursuing innovation by adding features (and the systems supporting them) was harming our quality performance, our customer retention – and sustainable profitable growth. As we scaled up, we now saw that new features and systems must integrate with existing ones to continue to provide a smooth and seamless experience for customers and staff. As a result, we put several "innovation" projects on hold (and downright cancelled a few) while we worked on making work the mess we'd created.

This triggered a long and healthy debate between us: would this stop innovation altogether? On the one hand, we could all agree that adding yet one more feature without making it work with what was already there would not help performance. On the other, focusing only on small-step improvements might hamstring our innovative capability terminally – after all, we had successfully built the company from scratch by bringing feature after feature to the market. In the end, our deeper understanding of innovation as adoption leads to a completely different innovation map. This is evident as we look at features historically: 1) we purchase a car for you at the best price, 2) you choose the

car you need on the website or mobile app, 3) you final-
ize a purchase at an outlet close to you, 4) you also can
purchase quality-guaranteed secondhand cars, 5) re-
sell your old car, 6) get all the paperwork done through
our service, 7) finance your car purchase, and 8) get the
car delivered to your door.

	Technology	Value analysis	Value engineering	Marketing
Purchasing	Look for tech innovations that radically reduce the cost of doing something and search for opportunities to change how we do things accordingly to deliver more value to customers.	Solve all small problems continuously with our existing services to better integrate systems, and learn how to make things work. This is a people capability in need of constant development.	Actively look for opportunities where both tech insight and production improvements can visibly improve performance and prepare new features accordingly.	Establish a rhythm of announcements to the market by investing in and promoting either small gains on existing services (facelifts) or introduction of breakthrough new features.
Online store				
Outlet				
Cars				
Repurchase				
Paperwork				
Home delivery				
Finance				

Seeing our scale-up as a flow of steady innovation,
both large and small, we realize more than ever that
this is not the work of one or two persons, no matter
how talented or smart, but of all people all the time: we
don't have a crystal ball, so we don't know from where
the next breakthrough idea is going to come. Furthermore, in creating value, we've found out that there is

rarely a clear "aha!" moment as we'd experienced in the early days (e.g., discovering that the deposit asked of customers blew their credit card limit). In fact, the more we practice, the more ideas emerge from ongoing, unformed, and sometimes contentious discussions about challenges and how we're responding to them.

The literature abounds with debates on "resistance to change." We've never encountered any. What we have found is that people are legitimately unsure of which step to take when the desired direction isn't explained clearly – or its logic. The logic we've now established is:

1. We aim to facilitate car purchases (as opposed to "sell cars") to the point that buying a car online becomes fully adopted by the market as a normal thing to do.

2. By satisfying every customer, every day (including in difficult periods)

3. Which means involving everyone every day on solving quality and cost issues

4. So that we better integrate systems and give our customers and frontline staff enabling tools to do the job (buying a car for customers, facilitating purchase for staff)

5. And find genuine opportunities for innovation by blending what we know how to do with new creative ideas.

The logic of this strategy is not always clear to all our staff, and so we, as leaders, need to demonstrate it and explain it at the workplace every day until all people see where they can participate and help – and find meaning in what they do. The more we progress, the more we see there is no real difference between strategy and execution. There is seeing and facing key challenges and then encouraging people to work on those as they do their day-to-day job, and as they work at improving their own current performance. The company as a whole is innovative if every person in it understands the overall direction and is supported in trying out creative ideas.

Solutions and innovations are not *executed*. They are formed into a value proposition for customers by everyone pitching in. To create an innovative organization, we need to move the company from a single breakthrough innovation and execution scale-up to an ongoing stream of innovation that takes advantage of technology opportunities. As leaders, we found this meant adopting a worldview of find problems, face obstacles, frame challenges, and form solutions. This also means that as leaders, we must shift our stance and develop a new skill set:

Sole problem solver	>	Listener of everyone
Decisive decider	>	Challenger of status quo through kaizen
Action plan controller	>	Orchestrator of teamwork
Spin communicator	>	Supporter of others' initiatives

CONCLUSION

We succeed when the people around us succeed: our customers, our staff, our suppliers. Lean has given us a framework to pursue this goal at scale.

First, lean relentlessly orients everyone's minds towards satisfying customers and looking at value from customers' points of view rather than putting internal convenience or self-interest first. Then it offers down-to-earth tools to put "problems first": visualize problems, discuss and define them, and review our analyses to sharpen our thinking. This enables us to collaborate more intensely on solutions that work for everyone and will satisfy customers while reducing the overall burden of cost on the business. Last but not least, visual systems – such as kanbans, andons, A3s, problem-solving boards, and suggestions follow-up – enable us to go and talk directly to people and ask ourselves the key question: "How can I help this person succeed?" Competence without care will not give us the sustainable growth we want. The real magic lies in *sharing* the solving of problems together – and appreciating every person for their contribution to our collective success.

From zero to 1 billion. From a phone and a desktop computer to operations in four countries. Our intuition of taking away customer pain points from the car-purchasing experience has paid off spectacularly. We have been incredibly lucky. We have ridden the wave of hypergrowth and – so far – surfed it without falling off the board. Yet, reality exists; reality resists. From idea to make it so is never easy. We have learned the hard way that capabilities are the product of competences and resources. For 20 years, we have been continuously working at developing both.

From the start, we knew that "learn or die" would be the key to success, but we had no idea what we needed to learn. The first hard lesson we had to face was that digital automation wasn't a panacea. It worked fabulously in our early years, adding customer features and internal systems as we grew, but then we hit the complexity wall. Systems add up, overlap, interact, and require increasingly difficult human trade-offs, just as the organization grows, splits into silos, and also becomes more complex and more rigid. In the early days, we thought that innovation would pull us through; as long as we pursued breakthroughs, we would be all right.

Indeed, we have been fortunate to personally ride three disruptive innovation waves: first, using the digital revolution to transform how customers purchase cars; second, joining the circular economy by creating industrial capabilities to refurbish cars and reuse them as "almost" new; and third, participating in the current drive to replace fuel-powered automobiles with electric engines. We've also learned that *breakthrough* innovation also requires incremental innovation – like two strands of a DNA chain. Without *incremental* efforts to improve and make it work, disruptive innovations often remain ideas without either competencies or resources to turn them into real-life capabilities. Many people had the idea of selling cars over the internet in the early 2000s – but we made it work. The same happened with circular-economy ideas, and we're seeing it again with electrification. Reality fights back, but ideas become commonplace practices if we can succeed in engaging and coordinating thousands of people in making it work for customers.

Conversely, following the path of incremental innovation without seeking breakthrough, disruptive innovation leaves you stranded with a service or product progressively out of line with customer expectations and markets. The surprise for us was to discover that the buds of ideas for disruptive insights are often generated in incremental innovation if you know how to seek them out, nurture them at the early ugly-duckling stage, and put in the necessary resources to reach lift-off. Innovations must first convince internally, then be adopted locally until they reach wider markets – it's a journey.

In the end, the real bottleneck to growth is the limited span of management focus. As you add customer features and the internal systems to support them, complexity increases exponentially, and management gets daily drawn into fighting fires and reacting to events rather than leading them. Regardless of how brilliant you are, there are only so many topics you can focus on in earnest at any one time. The only way around this bottleneck is to abandon central control of everything and to trust in the collective intelligence of all people in the company – not a natural reflex for entrepreneurs who've built everything with their bare hands, so to speak. To be more precise, the deeper challenge is to learn what needs to be rigorously controlled centrally and what needs to be opened up and released to local ideas and initiatives.

We'd been interested in lean thinking as an alternative to traditional leadership and management from the get-go, but meeting true senseis opened our eyes (and our minds) and completely changed our approach to leadership. We learned to be wary of our entrepreneurial reflex of sizing up situations at a glance, quickly defining the problem, coming up decisively with an (apparently) smart solution, and then driving it through the ranks – only to have unexpected consequences blow up in our faces and require endless effort to fix. With the senseis, we learned to more actively seek and *find* problems at the workplace by meeting people and seeing how they work, listening to what they thought, and taking their views and issues seriously. We needed to give people a *voice*.

In doing so, we relearned the basics of analysis: scoping the size of the problem, breaking it down into factors, and then asking ourselves the hard questions: which factors do we know, which don't we know. This *"face"* moment – facing factors you know little about or understand poorly – is the key to getting to grips with what you think can't be done (because you don't know how to do it right away) and the true, first step in innovative thinking. We were familiar with this feeling in large tech gambits, but we eventually learned to extend it to any difficult situation. The deep question here is: how long does it take us, as an organization, to face a problem, to realize we're backsliding, or that we're working around a difficult concern simply because it's difficult?

Face leads to *frame:* learning to express clearly and simply the gap between where you are and where you want to be in a way that anyone in the business can understand and, thus, contribute to in their own way. Framing orients. It clarifies the direction while leaving room for interpretation in different contexts and with different sets of eyes. A good frame liberates everyone to interpret the statement in the light of their own responsibility and come up with their own initiatives and their own plans – which we can then support. This pivot in our leadership attitude had the unexpected benefit of changing the work atmosphere throughout the company. As people grew more comfortable with revealing and discussing problems, they also relaxed (we discovered how much tension our frustration with the business scale-up issues was causing) and became far more engaged with their work and initiatives. Our internal satisfaction scores shot up, staff turnover slowed, and the place became, well, simply more fun to work in. When the pandemic hit, this new work culture became a lifesaving asset as our teams coped with the many huge challenges with courage and flexible thinking that awed us.

Framing allows you to *form* solutions across the organization. Local initiatives can be tested, checked, and, more importantly, shared – then improved. Teamwork is continuously strengthened as people share the changes they intend to carry out and the results of their attempts so we can collectively keep the *try-fail-analyze-try-again* discussion going and, progressively, issues clarify, people reach consensus on problems, and implementation is painless and fast because we already have buy-in.

Forming is a different form of leadership in which you constantly repeat and explain the problem, listen to what people intend to try as countermeasures, and organize the sharing of these experiments across silos. We started with a vision of hierarchy and subordination (who tells whom to do what) and different management techniques, such as setting up a community of practice across the business. We ended up with clearer understanding of collaboration (who talks to whom about what). A fast-growing organization is shaped far more than it's organized. Hypergrowth, we realized, is more pottery than architecture. It also relies more on people's individual initiatives – everyone every day – than simply on making the right calls and investing in the right tech. Our fast growth is clearly sustained by the fact that people largely like working in a place where they see what they're expected to achieve, their concerns are heard, and their ideas supported.

The deepest insight from our lean journey is probably the importance of maintaining a kaizen spirit through thick and thin and surrounding ourselves with growth-mindset managers. As problems increase and multiply, it's always so tempting to look for someone who'll take charge, bring order and control to the mess, and get things done. We've learned that although this looks good for a couple of months, it often ends in disaster. Growth-mindset people tend to not look so good as they immerse themselves in the problem, but then they learn – they learn what to do with others, not to others. In the end, the difference in outcome is spectacular, and we can see this every day.

Lastly, we've come to completely change our minds about lean. We were confused in our early days when talking to senseis because they were using the same analysis tools we'd tried before, but every time with a different twist, a different angle we couldn't quite fathom. Then we got it. The lean tools are not about doing something to people. They are about giving practical, concrete reference points for *self-assessment* and from then on for *self-improvement.* In many ways, the digital revolution has enabled companies to spread Taylorist thinking to every job. The process is defined by an expert, coded in a system and an app, and employees have to put data into cells and hit "next."

Much like driving by following the instructions of the GPS or Waze without knowing where you're going, digital Taylorism creates a world of constant reaction and very little planning or reflecting. It's seductive precisely because it saves you from thinking too much about how to move ahead, but it turns out it's also profoundly unsatisfying, a risk of burnout – and simply inefficient as people stop thinking of all the specifics of every case and lose their ability for good judgment. The lean alternative focuses on people's autonomy. It clarifies what we need to look at, what we need to decide, and then self-reflection on how these decisions turned out. Working this way daily is the key to self-reliance, greater trust in oneself and one's colleagues, and a collective spirit of collective achievement and personal accomplishment.

In his first visit in our refurbishment factory, one of our senseis asked of every car: "Why is it not at the next step?" He told us later that he also asked himself of every person he met: "Why is she not at the next grade?" We're getting there. We now look at people and their reactions and wonder: What are they looking at? How can they assess their own ability? What are they working on to improve? How can we better orient and support them? Indeed, the promise of lean to align individual fulfillment and corporate destiny is even clearer to us now that we grow across countries and cultures and invest more deeply in a circular economy. Early on, the challenge to combine individual benefit, business success, and benefit to society seemed like blue-sky thinking, but it now makes concrete, here-and-now sense. We grasp how this is precisely the way to balance the needs of today and tomorrow and build tomorrow's success on today's performance. And, indeed, if we can keep that balance, the sky is no limit.

INDEX

Printed in Poland
by Amazon Fulfillment
Poland Sp. z o.o., Wrocław

10437092R00237